Praise
LOST and

"For a decade, I have been honored to work with ⌐⌐⌐ ⌐⌐⌐⌐ ⌐⌐ Smith on development issues in the Democratic Republic of the Congo. He brings the same honesty, focus, and thoughtfulness to his day job as he does to addressing the complexities of chronic pain and mental illness. His personal battle with both, told in a brave and easy-to-understand chronicle of his journey, is a valuable tool and useful guide for the millions in our country facing these same issues. *Lost and Broken* helps advance a long overdue effort to talk more openly about, and find better solutions for, both chronic pain and mental illness."

—**Ben Affleck,** director, actor, and
co-founder Eastern Congo Initiative

"With this book, Adam tackles the stigma around mental health in the most effective way possible, by being honest and revealing about his own battles with anxiety and chronic pain, showing that even the most accomplished among us can struggle. Our family knows all too well what it is to get knocked down and have a hard time getting up again, and we were lucky enough to have a friend like Adam then. This book is the caring resource that anyone in that position can draw wisdom and support from."

—**Senator Mark Kelly and former
Congresswoman Gabby Giffords**

"*Lost and Broken* is a courageous book chronicling Congressman Adam Smith's personal journey through debilitating anxiety and chronic pain. Adam offers an honest and accessible window into the transformative powers of non-judgmental curiosity about our own suffering; a willingness to experiment with new tools and habits; perseverance; and ultimately, self-love. In the process, he highlights how misaligned today's healthcare system is both for healing the chronic health challenges that afflict hundreds of millions of Americans and for building our collective resilience."

—**Elizabeth A. Stanley, PhD,** Georgetown University
professor and author of *Widen the Window: Training Your Brain
and Body to Thrive During Stress and Recover from Trauma*

"When I started reading *Lost and Broken*, I could not stop. This book tells the vulnerable and unfortunately typical story of Representative Adam Smith's struggles with anxiety and chronic pain. Smith reveals the lengths he went to both treat and hide these struggles, and the consistent hurdles of poor treatment and lousy information he encountered. In doing so, his compelling book provokes the right questions: how do people in emotional and physical pain figure out what works, and how do those with less access to resources and support even stand a chance?"

—**Lynn Lyons, LICSW,** author of *The Anxiety Audit*,
coauthor of *Anxious Kids, Anxious Parents*

LOST
and
BROKEN

My Journey Back from Chronic Pain
and Crippling Anxiety

LOST
and
BROKEN

Congressman Adam Smith

Health Communications, Inc.
Boca Raton, Florida

www.hcibooks.com

Library of Congress Cataloging-in-Publication Data
is available through the Library of Congress

ISBN-13: 978-07573-2462-8 (Paperback)
ISBN-10: 0-7573-2462-2 (Paperback)
ISBN-13: 978-07573-2463-5 (ePub)
ISBN-10: 0-7573-2463-0 (ePub)

Publisher: Health Communications, Inc.
301 Crawford Boulevard, Suite 200
Boca Raton, FL 33432–3762

Cover, interior design, and typesetting by Larissa Hise Henoch

To Alan and Kirk,
thank you beyond words
for your dedication to finding ways
to help people in your chosen fields
of mental health and muscle
activation therapy.

CONTENTS

CHAPTER 7

CHAPTER 8

CHAPTER 9

CHAPTER 10

CHAPTER 11

CHAPTER 12

CHAPTER 13

CHAPTER 14

CHAPTER 15

CHAPTER 16

CHAPTER 17

CHAPTER 18

CHAPTER 19

CHAPTER 20

CHAPTER 21

CHAPTER 22

CHAPTER 23

CHAPTER 24

CHAPTER 25

CHAPTER 26

CHAPTER 27

CHAPTER 28

ACKNOWLEDGMENTS

I am grateful for all the people who helped me in so many ways during my battle with anxiety and chronic pain. It would take a lot of space to list them all, and I would inevitably leave out some, so I will just give one big, incredibly heartfelt *Thank-You!* to one and all while taking a brief moment to mention a few who really stood out.

Paul Arcangeli and the incredible team that he led for so many years on the House Armed Services Committee. Shana Chandler and the equally incredible team she led on my congressional staff. Jon Pawlow, Debra Entenman, Matthew Perry (not that one), Salem Miriam, Sarah Servin, Brian Garrett, Katy Quinn, Michael Amato, Paul Hoover, and Alex Stone: all good friends and outstanding public servants. Michael Herson, Rick Jones, Calvin Goings, and Tom and Jenny Rosetto were also outstanding sounding boards and good and supportive friends, then and now.

And, of course, my wife, Sara, and my children, Kendall and Jack. Close family members come along for journeys like mine and really don't have much choice in the matter, but I couldn't have made it through my struggles without the love and support of them all. I am beyond lucky and blessed to have these three amazing people in my life.

Lost and Broken itself came about because of the help and support of a number of people. First, going way back, Peter Rex voluntarily took on the unenviable task of helping me learn how to write almost thirty years ago while I was messing around with a novel I was trying to complete. I finished it, and though it never went further than that, the years-long process of working on it, and Peter's willingness to help edit numerous iterations, really helped me in being able to write this book.

Michael Herson was the first one to assist me in my effort to get Lost and Broken published. He helped send the book out to prospective literary agents. Mel Berger is the one who picked up that challenge and is responsible for finding the book's publisher, Health Communications, Inc. (HCI). Mel is incredibly knowledgeable and diligent, and has been a tremendous advocate for the book. And lastly, I want to thank Christine Belleris and Lindsey Mach at HCI for being such great partners in bringing Lost and Broken to print.

CHAPTER 1
Rock Bottom
APRIL 2016

I woke up one morning in early April of 2016 and seriously considered the possibility that I might never be able to get out of bed. Could I ever find the strength, courage, and focus to just get up? Crippling anxiety, chronic pain, muscle atrophy, and an increasingly confusing mix of pharmaceuticals coursing through my body had brought me to this point of doubt. I felt broken and pathetic. A part of me knew this was ridiculous. I had to get up, and I also knew that in the literal sense of it, I was capable of getting out of bed.

But my life terrified me. What would I do if I got up? How bad would the pain be? Could I get my mind to calm down enough to focus on any particular task? How long could I stand? Sit? Walk? Should I take an extra dose of my anti-anxiety meds? Pain meds? The mere thought of having to make these decisions sent a surge of even greater anxiety through me. Then I thought about the consequences of simply staying in bed. I could almost physically feel my muscles getting weaker by the moment from all the inactivity, and they were already weak enough. If I didn't get up, surely the day would come when I really, honest to God, physically couldn't.

It was getting increasingly difficult to decide, which terrified me more—getting up or staying in bed.

Then I thought about my job. My third hip surgery—total replacement of my left hip—had been in February in Seattle, two months ago. I hadn't been back to DC since. This meant I had missed a lot of votes. How many? I had no idea. Too many. That I knew. I had hoped for a six-week recovery. Now, I had no clue. I was lying in my bed worrying about just getting up and out of that bed. How in the hell was I ever going to get on an airplane and do the five-and-a-half-hour flight back to DC? Much less find a way to do my job and keep flying back and forth.

And reelection was coming. In November. Every two years, whether I liked it or not, I used to like to joke. Filing was a month away, and nobody had yet decided to run against me. But there were rumors. There were always rumors. This was another of my pithy observations from my previous life. Thinking and talking about running for office is always a hell of a lot more fun than actually doing it. But what if, this time, somebody serious actually did do it? Again, how could I possibly run a campaign in my current physical and mental state?

"I just can't do it," I said quietly to myself. "I'm not going to make it." I had said this more times than I could count by this point, even though I still didn't know exactly what it meant.

I did eventually get up. And slowly, unevenly, and painfully I found a way back. I learned a lot during this journey. I want to share what I learned in the hope that it can help people facing similar problematic healthcare challenges. I will use the rest of this opening chapter to offer the main takeaways up front. I've always been a big fan of executive summaries.

Executive Summary

First, we must eliminate the stigma in this country surrounding mental illness. That stigma makes it far harder for people facing mental illness to take the first step we all need to take. Get help. Seek treatment. It really does work. There are treatments that work and that can dramatically improve your mental health. Too many people still try to hide these problems, afraid that others will judge them for it; that people will treat them differently; that they will lose their jobs, friends, or family.

My most recent battle with crippling anxiety started in March of 2013. My chronic physical pain didn't begin to become debilitating until July of 2014.

I vividly remember thinking, as the pain got worse, *Well, now at least I have something socially acceptable wrong with me. I don't have to completely lie about why I'm not feeling up to a trip or a social event, or why I can't do as much work as I ordinarily would. My hips hurt, and the pain is too bad to sit or stand for long. Yeah, that works. Much better than saying, you know, I really can't explain it. My heart's going a million miles an hour, I can't sleep, I feel like I need to jump out of my own skin, I think I'm having a bad reaction to the Benzos I've been on for the last year, and maybe I shouldn't have tried to wean myself off of them just yet, so, hey, sorry, I have to stay in and focus on the latest panic attack. I can't make the caucus retreat in Williamsburg as planned.*

Cliche as it may be, the first step to dealing with a problem is admitting you have one. If social pressure stops us from admitting to a mental illness, then we won't take that first step to seek help. We won't get the treatment we need to get better.

Second, psychotherapy works. I resisted this at first. I mean, "psycho" therapy? Okay, I've got some issues, but I'm not a psycho. Yes, I was just that ignorant.

Psychotherapy works by helping us open up and examine our past. Talking about it really does help. It helps us better understand our emotions, like anger and guilt. The source of these emotions is likely much deeper than what we believe to be the immediate cause. Issues from as far back as our childhood can upset us long after they occurred. And these issues don't have to be as severe or traumatic as one might think.

Psychotherapy is not a cure-all, and it works differently for different people, but it helped me, and I urge others to try it. I best understood the treatment when I read the following quote from psychologist Alice Miller: "The aim of therapy is not to correct the past. It is to help the patient to confront his own history, and to grieve over it." Psychotherapy can also help you better understand how to address issues that might be going on in your life right now, things you find frustrating for one reason or another but that you have not honestly assessed.

The bottom line here is that it can be helpful to have someone guide us to honestly and openly talk about important issues in our lives, past and present.

Third, do not underestimate the impact of individual mental health issues, even seemingly minor ones, on the level of conflict and instability in our society. Mental health issues give rise to anger, fear, and frustration, and those emotions spill out of people in unpredictable ways that often lead to conflict.

Think about the people you interact with in everyday life who seem unnecessarily angry and disagreeable. The neighbors who get into an epic fight over exactly how and where the fence should be built between their two properties and who should pay for it. The person on an airplane who gets angry and insults the flight attendant because she just ran out of Diet Sprite. The TSA agent who barks at you and makes you feel inept because you didn't step out of the body scanner quickly enough. Sorry, I spend a lot of time in airports and on airplanes. But you get the idea. Road rage on the highway. Angry people in line at the grocery store. Fist fights at youth sports events. It happens everywhere.

I used to have a simple, straightforward thought when I witnessed somebody having this type of disagreeable, angry reaction.

What a jackass.

Now, after my own struggles with mental illness and pain, I far more often wonder what is going on with this excessively angry person. Do they have anxiety? Pain? Depression? What unresolved issues from their past might be causing their disproportionate anger, fear, and frustration in the present? What might be going on in the person's life right now that could be causing it?

Our hyper-capitalist, winner-takes-all country has a tendency to take these situations where people have anger, fear, and frustration from things going on in their lives past or present, and throw more fuel on that fire in an effort to benefit particular interests. The media, propelled by the twenty-four-hour news cycle that needs to be filled with "breaking news," tries to make us fearful and angry so we will watch, read, or listen to them for solutions, thereby benefitting these outlets by retaining or gaining revenue from corporate sponsors. Political groups feed on that anger, fear, and frustration, using various means to show us how one group of people, or some trend in our society, is threatening our very existence. The only way to preserve what we hold most dear in our lives in the face of this threat? Send them just one more contribution.

The easiest products to sell in America are fear and outrage, and I firmly believe that part of the reason for that is the number of people struggling with anger, fear, and frustration driven by underlying mental health issues that have not been addressed.

Fourth, you cannot solely rely on doctors or other healthcare providers to solve your healthcare problem. I failed to understand, for far too long, the degree to which I needed to take responsibility for my own diagnosis and treatment. I didn't want to do that. I was scared, blindsided by pain and anxiety that I had no idea how to address. I didn't want to do the hard work necessary to think through a difficult problem. I wanted somebody to fix me, to tell me what was wrong with me, and then to tell me exactly what I had to do to make it disappear. And I wanted an exact timeline. Take these pills, get these procedures, do these exercises—and in three months you will be cured!

It doesn't work that way.

Ironically, I had always been a big believer in the principle of hard work and the willingness to think through difficult problems. I loved to quote a line from a Sue Grafton mystery novel to make my point: "Thinking's hard work, which is why you don't see many people doing it." I had always prided myself on taking the opposite approach, thinking my way to better results in my job, in sports, in most aspects of my life. I wasn't the best student or the best athlete. I didn't come from money or a prominent family. I believed I had to work harder, think more, and find solutions. But when it came to confronting my anxiety and chronic pain, I froze. I did not see a way out.

Unfortunately, my outlook on this issue didn't change the basic truth that it is the rare doctor or healthcare provider who will completely take control of a patient's diagnosis and treatment. We patients have to fight through the fear and push them for better answers, more detailed analysis, and, where necessary, more thoughtful and creative solutions.

Fifth, the complexity of the human body and mind makes the process of diagnosis and treatment far more difficult than it may at first appear. If healthcare providers could take a patient and easily diagnose the exact cause of the problematic symptoms and then know the correct treatment given that diagnosis, that would be one thing. But no two patients are exactly the same. Subtle differences in symptoms can be enormously important. Patients, even if they have the same basic ailment or disease, can react very differently to treatments administered. And, for all the progress we have made, there is still a frighteningly large amount that modern science doesn't know about what can go wrong with the human body and how to fix it.

I developed a liver ailment in early 2002, long before my more complicated health problems confronted me. I was extremely fatigued and had night sweats, so I visited my doctor's office. Bloodwork revealed very elevated enzymes in my liver. Then they ran tests. I did not have any form of hepatitis or any other of the more obvious liver diseases. Eventually they gave me a diagnosis. I quickly forgot the disease name they told me. But I accepted it. I felt bad, went to the doctor, got examined, and they diagnosed what was wrong with me. It was an infection that would go away with time, and it did.

Only that wasn't actually what happened. I looked deeper into this liver problem once my later experience gave me cause for greater skepticism about any given medical diagnosis. The disease name they gave me wasn't actually a specific diagnosed disease. It was, quite simply, the name doctors back in 2002 gave to patients with elevated liver enzymes and mild symptoms when those doctors had absolutely no idea what had caused the elevated enzymes in the first place or what exactly was now wrong with the patient's liver. The symptoms did go away, but my liver enzymes remain elevated to this day, though not nearly as elevated as they were initially. The more honest answer from my doctor would have been "I have no idea what caused your current symptoms, and don't have any suggestions on how to treat it. Odds are it will get better."

The more I learned about medical problems, the more I realized this wasn't an isolated example. Symptoms and abnormal test results frequently do not lead to a specific diagnosis. Doctors find clues and can act on those clues, but specific, definitive conclusions are frequently elusive.

The problems that brought me to a state of near immobility in April 2016 involved a complex mix of functional breakdowns in my brain, muscles, skeletal system, and nervous system—a series of mind-numbingly complicated interworking systems about which modern medicine still has much to learn. Prescribing the right course of action in confronting healthcare problems like this is almost never easy. It requires a robust system of critical thinking and problem-solving, a relentless ability to challenge assumptions and seek answers that may not appear obvious at first glance, and an ability to gather all the details possible to help in this problem-solving process.

Sixth, our healthcare system in America is not well designed for the type of critical thinking and complex problem-solving that many healthcare challenges require. I found this frustrating. And that sentence is the greatest understatement you will read in this book.

In March of 2013, when debilitating anxiety hit me, I reached out to my contacts at the University of Washington to find a psychologist. They made a recommendation, and I met with this person twice. It didn't help. From that point until April of 2018, as I navigated through anxiety, chronic pain, and three hip surgeries, including two total replacements, I saw over one hundred healthcare providers—internists, osteopaths, psychiatrists, psychologists, physical therapists, personal trainers, massage therapists, chiropractors, acupuncturists, naturopaths, and undoubtedly a few other specialties I can't now recall. The fact that I saw that many people tells you how well the system worked for me.

Admittedly, some of this was my fault. Early on, I wanted the quick fix, and I didn't even begin to understand exactly what help I needed. I should have given that psychologist at UW Medicine more than two bites at the apple, for example. But the system itself is deeply flawed. Somebody blindsided by debilitating anxiety and severe chronic pain is unlikely to be thinking clearly. These conditions shouldn't make it almost impossible for patients to get the help they need. I have also listened to enough other people who have faced healthcare challenges of their own to know that my difficulties were more the norm than some kind of outlier.

So, flawed how?

For starters, the economic incentives push healthcare providers away from the type of in-depth, critical-thinking approach needed to deal with the sheer complexity of the human body and everything that can and does go wrong with it. Our healthcare system pays for quantity, not quality. It pays for tests, procedures, surgeries, visits, and drugs. Providers of healthcare products and services get paid the same, in almost all cases, whether that given product or service helps the patient or not. Family physicians do not get paid more if they see a patient for longer. This discourages any sort of in-depth analysis of what is wrong with the patient and the pros and cons of a given treatment approach. Surgeries and tests are usually well compensated, so they get ordered. Once a given specialty figures out how insurance companies pay for a given treatment, that healthcare specialty goes to great lengths to maximize the income from offering that treatment.

A major hospital in Seattle got dinged by regulators for having a single brain surgeon perform up to three brain surgeries at the same time, triple billing for what, I assume, was only a slightly larger time investment by the surgeon. And there's a reason the training to become a chiropractor contains a fair amount of explanation as to how patients get billed and exactly how insurance companies pay for services provided.

Another problem grows out of these economic incentives. Healthcare providers get very comfortable in what they do. They get very uncomfortable when confronted with new information suggesting that what they do really shouldn't be done anymore. Try showing an orthopedic surgeon updated information that suggests joint replacements are currently being done on patients who don't really need them. Or telling a physical therapist that new studies on muscles show that his miracle-cure ten-week treatment plan (which fits comfortably within the number of visits and treatments insurance will pay for) doesn't actually work.

Harry Truman once said, "An expert is someone who is afraid to learn anything new because then he wouldn't be an expert anymore." Again, this outlook hinders the ability of healthcare providers to deal with the complexity of the human body and to keep up with all the new information coming in on how to treat it.

Complex problem-solving also requires a collaborative process, and in the case of healthcare problems, this means patients and providers working together. Healthcare providers tend to be bad at this. They don't really listen to patients in any great depth, and they don't spend much time figuring out how to be sure they are communicating clearly with their patients. Much of this is a time issue. Remember, doctors rarely get paid more for spending more time with patients. Doctors also, I believe, approach their profession more like a physical scientist or an engineer than like a social scientist, really examining how to communicate with people or how people process information.

In November of 2009, my right lung collapsed. I didn't know this at the time, of course. All I knew was that when I woke up that morning the right side of my chest hurt like hell, and breathing had suddenly become very difficult. I paid a visit to the House physician's office in the US Capitol, and they couldn't come up with an explanation for the symptoms (very troubling in its own regard, but not the point of this story). I went back to my office and nearly decided to just suck it up and fly home, all the way across the country, as planned. Instead, I took another trip to the House physician's office, and this time they sent me to what was then Bethesda Naval Hospital for a CT scan.

I got there, checked in, and eventually found myself lying down while the machine around me worked its magic. I barely had time to lie down when, after just a couple of minutes, the technician came back in the room and said, "They want you to go to the emergency room." I got up and followed him. He said nothing else. We walked down the hallway, turning corners here and there, for a minute or two before I finally decided to speak. "Uh, not to be overly nosy here, but just out of curiosity, why do they want me to go to the emergency room?"

"Your right lung is 75 percent collapsed," he said as he kept walking.

I took a few more steps before saying, "And I'm guessing that's a bad thing."

He might have looked at me at this point. Maybe even cracked a small smile. I don't recall. But in my healthcare experiences to come, I thought back on this trip to Bethesda as perfectly indicative of how people who work in healthcare communicate with their patients.

Seventh, don't give up on science, logic, and reason. Persist. Fight through the bad information, the doubts, the false starts, the completely contradictory information two supposedly expert doctors give you days apart, and keep searching for ways to improve your health and for the answers to what ails your body and mind. Help exists, even if it doesn't come easily.

This, too, I doubted. It seemed pointless. I would commit to one course of treatment only to find it didn't work—over and over again. People kept telling me, "Two steps forward, one step back," when, to me, it felt like it was the other way around. What was the point in seeing one more doctor, psychologist, or physical therapist? Nothing worked. But I was learning, even if it didn't feel that way, as a very good friend of mine told me, everything is a data point. If you try something and it doesn't work, that outcome provides information. Learn from it.

The human body is resilient. Help can usually be found. It isn't easy, and you have to think your way through the process, but you can find treatments and healthcare providers who can help. Modern healthcare, for all it has not yet learned and for all its faults and limitations, still has come a long way. Never stop looking for those answers.

CHAPTER 2
A Mental Block on Mental Illness

was thirty-nine years old before I would consider the possibility of mental illness in my life. Even then, during the six-month battle with severe anxiety that hit me that year, I viewed it as an aberration. I thought it was like when I had mumps and chicken pox as a child—really weird and disconcerting but something that would just go away at some point.

Oddly, it wasn't like I'd never had to talk to anybody about mental health issues. I worked in politics. I had been elected to the Washington State Senate at age twenty-five and the US Congress at thirty-one. I regularly met with mental health advocates. We discussed the need for greater public policy support for people with mental health issues and the importance of increasing funding for mental health services. Several times a year I had these meetings. I strongly supported the efforts of these advocates.

Sometime in the early 2000s, one of these meetings was wrapping up when one of the advocates asked a final question. "Have you or anyone in your family ever had a mental health issue?"

I paused for a second before saying, "Uh, no." My hesitation wasn't because I was wondering about what the correct answer was. I hesitated because the first thing that popped into my head was an emphatic "Of course not," and I could sense by the way the woman had asked the question that such a dismissive answer wasn't going to go over well. I had to at least appear like I didn't think the question had such an obvious answer in the negative.

I just didn't think of mental illness as applying to a "normal" person like me. Mental illness was *One Flew over the Cuckoo's Nest*. It was the guy at the bus stop, rocking back and forth and mumbling to himself about the power of the Lord almighty. It was Ted Bundy. Son of Sam. You know, crazy people.

I was wrong about that. "Normal" people struggle with mental illness all the time, and what constitutes normal in the first place is something none of us should be so quick to judge. That raises the question: what does rise to the level of being considered a "mental health issue"? And the follow-up: what exactly needs to be happening to you for you to decide to seek help?

It helps, in answering these questions, to consider them from the perspective of what one does in response to physical health issues and to understand that in both cases the answer is not always easy.

Health, both physical and mental, at the most basic level involves two sets of decisions—treatment and prevention. Ouch, that hurts! Do I need to do something about it? And, if I take these actions, maybe then I won't wind up in pain or discomfort in the first place?

You have a headache. It could be a tumor but probably not. You don't immediately get an MRI. You either ride it out or take some over-the-counter pain medication. This example combines my two basic points. First, don't ignore healthcare problems. Address them and take appropriate action. Second, appropriate action requires thought. The amount of thought will vary depending on the problem, but both our bodies and our healthcare system are complicated enough that we all need to spend at least some time considering how to address the healthcare challenges facing us.

The easiest example on prevention is going to the dentist. You get your teeth cleaned twice a year, right? In this case, you don't go to the dentist because something is wrong. You go to make it less likely something will go wrong. I learned the truth of preventative dental care during college when, for a variety of reasons, I didn't visit a dentist for over three years. My teeth hurt like hell. Finally, when I could no longer ignore it, I made an appointment for a cleaning and checkup. This, too, hurt considerably as my dentist scraped over three years of plaque off of my teeth and out from under my gums, but then they felt better.

Now, do we have to do this twice a year? Maybe once a year would be fine, but the dental industry makes money off the visits and has convinced the public, and health insurers, twice is required. I don't really know. But I do know three years is too long. That brings us back to a basic question on mental health. What constitutes prudent prevention for mental health and what symptoms should cause us to seek help for a mental health issue? I struggled mightily to answer these questions for many reasons, but a big one was that, for a very long time, it didn't even occur to me to ask them. Physical problems? Sure. My knee hurts, I go see someone. I exercise and eat right to keep my body healthy in the first place. But stress is just stress, right? We all have stress and just live with it. I'm not crazy. Why would I worry about mental health?

CHAPTER 3
Crippling Anxiety

started worrying about my mental health in March of 2005. I lay in my bed in my home in Tacoma, Washington, gripped by a level of panic I had never before experienced. My heart pounded, and I literally felt like I was in mortal danger. Fear permeated by entire being. But fear of what? I kind of had an answer to that in one sense. The fear seemed focused on death.

Suddenly, the inevitability of my own death crept into my consciousness as the only thing worth focusing on in the world, and something that both completely and constantly terrorized me and that I had no idea how to handle. But this answer didn't seem quite right to me. First of all, the pulsating anxiety, the existential fear just hit me that night. I hadn't been thinking about death, and that specific idea didn't set in for several hours after the symptoms had kicked in. Plus, by this point in life I had thought about death many times. I didn't obsess over it, but I was certainly aware of it. So why now?

I had no idea. No great crisis had suddenly entered my life that I could identify. My life seemed fine. Yes, I had stress, but I was healthy, as were my wife and two children. I liked my job. I wasn't facing a personal financial crisis. The fear that possessed me came from nothing I could even begin to identify, and it wouldn't go away. Day after day, I remained in this state. I could barely force myself to eat, and sleep came only briefly and fitfully—if at all. What the hell?

How did I get to this place?

Modern life challenges most people. I don't know that my life at that point, a few months short of my fortieth birthday, was that unusual. I was married with two children, a four-year-old girl and a one-year-old boy. I represented the ninth district of the state of Washington in the US Congress, but my family chose to live in our home state, not Washington, DC. Clearly, working and living in two places on opposite sides of the country did complicate our lives. I logged over 100,000 air miles a year flying back and forth, and the schedule in Congress could be unpredictable, forcing difficult decisions on exactly when to catch which flight each way.

It is impossible to quickly explain when Congress is in session in DC and when it isn't—it can be five days a week, four, or even at times three on the weeks when we are in session.

Some months have a week or two set aside for district work periods when we are not in session those weeks, and in general we weren't in session in August and usually not that much in January or December, though this became less and less the case as politics got more complicated after roughly 2008. My wife and I mostly traveled back and forth together for my first two years in Congress, 1996–1998, spending some weekends in DC and some at home. For two years after that, my wife stayed mostly in Tacoma, and I flew back and forth almost every week. We went back to traveling back and forth together after our daughter was born in 2000, though with a vastly higher degree of difficulty, given that we had a small child with us. This changed in 2003 when our son was born. My wife and our children stayed at home in Tacoma, visiting DC a couple times a year, and I flew home whenever Congress wasn't voting, matching the above-described, complicated schedule.

But, again, if you have young children, you have a complicated life, one way or the other. I didn't think of my life as being unique in this regard. I did sense, however, as we headed into 2005, my stress level getting higher.

At that point, I thought of my life as a series of responsibilities, responsibilities I took very seriously—to my wife, to my children, to the people I was elected to represent, to the staff who worked for me, to the committees I served on in Congress, and to my colleagues—to just about everybody I encountered in my life. I had to find the time to meet those responsibilities. My approach to this challenge, and to the challenges that had come before that in my life, had always been somewhat complicated.

My whole life I was driven, ambitious. I wanted a lot out of life, and so I took on big challenges. Sometimes I did this with enthusiasm and humor. It was a game, and if I played it well, I could win. I reveled in finding a way to win, whether it was the tough campaigns I ran to get elected to the state Senate and then Congress or getting the kids fed, bathed, and in bed by the appointed time. I juggled meetings, flights, pediatrician appointments, phone calls, housework, and so forth, all with the objective of getting it done to the satisfaction of all those people to whom I felt responsible, and to achieve what I believed I needed to achieve in life.

Other times, meeting these challenges wore me down and frustrated me beyond belief. I felt angry at the obstacles thrown in my way, and guilty even thinking about the possibility that I might fail.

Way back in that first campaign for state Senate, I remember rushing through a series of phone calls one morning while getting my doorbelling literature ready for my afternoon precinct walk as I realized I was running late to get to a meeting I had with a labor union, which was considering giving me a contribution. I rushed out, got in my car, and started the drive. Only a few minutes into my journey, a traffic light turned yellow and forced me to brake to a stop. This minor delay lit a fuse of simmering rage. I pounded the steering wheel and let out a loud series of F-bombs with escalating anger and frustration before glancing at the lane next to me. Sitting calmly in his car, looking back at me with his mouth slightly agape, was my campaign manager, likely headed out for a series of his own errands. It was summer; neither of us had air conditioning in our cars, so our windows were down. There was no denying the tirade.

"Boss," he said by way of greeting and with mild concern in his voice.

"Jeffrey," I responded before looking back up at the offending traffic light and waiting awkwardly until it finally turned green.

My point is that I had some deep-seated anger and frustration boiling in me that took me decades to fully understand, and the more my life looked like I couldn't handle it anymore, couldn't achieve what I thought I was supposed to achieve, the more those issues bubbled to the surface at inopportune times.

Then there was the fear and insecurity, my near-constant companions as a child, and a consistent challenge in my life until about five months after my twenty-fifth birthday. This also didn't mix well with my very large ambitions, and it didn't make sense to me. How could I be so ambitious, wanting so much out of life, and at the same time be so utterly fearful of so many basic things?

Growing up, I was afraid of heights, water, loud noises, interacting with people I didn't know, and more things in general than I can list. My father couldn't believe how afraid I was of a razor when he tried to teach me how to shave. Needless to say, I had a major confidence problem. I simply didn't trust the world around me. Now, once I got comfortable in a situation, got some confidence, I could relax and engage. But that was not an easy place for me to get to for the first twenty-five years of my life.

Only two things seemed to help me get over these fears and frustrations, thus enabling me to slowly and awkwardly pursue those life ambitions—time, and just flat plowing through the fear when I determined it was either that or fail.

Time helped me in junior high school. The approaching first day of seventh grade terrified me. If I had any choice in the matter, I would have refused to go. Grade school was one thing. Same class and same teacher, all day, all year, and basically the same kids. Now, I had six separate classes, six different teachers, with a whole bunch of kids I didn't know. Resigned to my fate, I kept my head down, found the kids I did know from my grade school as well as from soccer and baseball, and slowly settled in over the course of the year.

Spanish class best illustrates how time helped me. I kept mostly quiet for the better part of seven months. I was studious and spoke only when I had to speak. Yes, those days when I had to make a presentation in front of the class had my stomach in knots for days leading up to them—as it likely did many other kids—but I bit the bullet and got through it. Then, finally, by mid-April I felt comfortable. This did not go unnoticed, particularly by my exasperated teacher, who one day, in response to some comment I had made, said for all the class to hear, "What happened to you, Antonio?" (my Spanish name for purposes of the class). "You used to be such a nice, quiet kid!"

I offered no answer, and at that point in my life would have struggled to explain it, even if I had felt so inclined. Give the teacher credit on this, though; her calling me out like that in front of the class caused my natural fear and lack of confidence to return and get me back in line—at least for a brief period of time. The answer, I later learned, went something like this, "Well, for complicated reasons, I'm shy and introverted in new situations. Takes me a long time to get comfortable. Once I get comfortable, my true self emerges, and, sorry, that true self is kind of a smart-ass and doesn't always follow rules like it should."

I didn't, however, always have time to slowly ease into new situations, especially given my life ambitions. My chosen strategy in these situations involved just jumping in, gritting my teeth, and getting through whatever challenge I had to confront for as long as I had to confront it until I could relax and get back to a more comfortable place. I worried my way through problems, physically forcing myself to absorb the stress as long as I could while always having a safe place to retreat to for periods of time to regain my strength.

My fourth-grade class spent a month getting bussed to a local indoor pool to take swimming lessons. I was having none of it. I refused to get into water over my head. Day after day, two other similarly frightened kids and I stood awkwardly on the side of the pool watching the rest of the students swim. Then one day, while our whole class stood on the pool deck getting instructions, I simply walked away from the group and jumped into twelve feet of water. Then I learned how to swim.

Relatively speaking, that was easy. It only required one brief moment of sucking it up and pushing through my fear. I never did get there playing baseball as a child. I was afraid of the ball. As I got older, the pitchers threw harder. At a certain point, I could either focus on the ball not hitting me or me hitting the ball. I couldn't do both. I didn't have time. My baseball-playing efforts, such as they were, nose-dived and officially ended at age fifteen.

The same might have happened with soccer except for a well-disguised lucky break. I played midfield my first couple years, ages seven and eight. I was okay, not great. I feared physical contact and played timidly. I attempted to hide out in the midfield, thinking there was enough going on that maybe people wouldn't notice my fear. In my third year, my team found itself without a goalie. I wasn't starting at that point, so in another moment of hard-to-explain daring, I volunteered.

Goalies can't hide. If you flinch, you lose. The ball goes into the goal, and everybody notices you messed up. I found my courage because of how much I hated losing. I had no choice. Suddenly I was no longer afraid on the soccer field. A couple of years later, I moved back to midfield, and, the fear gone, I turned into a good player.

My decision at age twenty-three, as I struggled through my second year of law school, to run for the state Senate created some obvious problems. It was another leap of faith, but unlike my jump into the pool, it would last for almost two years, not a few seconds. It helped that few people gave me any chance of winning and that back in 1990, campaigning was a simpler endeavor—no twenty-four-hour news, no Internet, a lot less money. I could hang out in the back room of my mother's house and plot and plan my campaign in relative peace and solitude. But, if I was going to win, I couldn't hang out back there forever.

Long story short, I figured it out. I won, and that victory gave me a surge of confidence that propelled me for a long time. I freaked out internally countless times during my campaign, but I always found just enough strength to keep going. I stressed beyond belief the few times I had to come into contact with my opponent. Fortunately, my opponent, a sixteen-year incumbent, didn't take me seriously, so she avoided such contact for reasons entirely different from mine.

I had doorbelled for other candidates before, but doing it for myself caused that same level of stress. So, one day in February of the election year, I just gathered up a stack of campaign literature, took a deep breath, walked out my front door, and knocked on every door on my street and then the next one and the next one after that. I slowly built a better system in the weeks and months that followed—precinct maps, lists of registered voters, and eventually got very comfortable with that type of campaigning.

I found that if I could force myself to go to meetings where I had the chance to speak to some audience or another about my campaign, just absorb the stress and start making my pitch, I could do a decent job and slowly relax a little.

Again, the idea that any of these issues I had meant I had a mental health issue I should deal with never even occurred to me. And I was lucky. I found workarounds for my anxiety. A whole lot of people struggle to a far greater extent. Some people have such profound social anxiety that they can't even leave their own house. But just because you aren't in that category doesn't mean that you might not have mental health issues that need to be addressed.

Me? I won. Upset of the year. I could, finally, after years of constant stress that my internal fears would stop me from achieving the life I felt destined to live, after all that time literally hating who I was, hating my place in the world (to quote Jerry McGuire), it was all good. Or so I thought at the time.

A psychologist I met in 2013, as I fought through the early stages of my latest anxiety flare-up, told me that it wasn't the

amount of stress in your life that exacerbates the anxiety. It was
the way you processed it. I found a lot of truth in this outlook.
Clearly, I processed stress poorly. I viewed too many things as
borderline existential threats, I worried excessively as I dealt
with those threats, and, as I later took to saying, I was the uncrowned king of regret—always beating myself up over the decisions I had made that had led to problems in my life. *If only* . . .
Why didn't I just . . . How could I be so stupid? Worry, worry, worry.
About the past. About the future. About everything I perceived
to threaten what I wanted out of life.

I honestly used to say to myself, *It's the stuff I don't worry*
about that gets me in trouble. There is a logic to this in one sense.
Thinking ahead and planning helps. Anticipating problems and
finding solutions doesn't just happen. One has to think or "worry" about the details. But I took this to a whole other level. I
honestly thought that the actual act of worrying protected me.
If I relaxed while confronting a problem, it would get me somehow. I didn't just have to think through it. I had to have the
physical feeling of being worried. Even bad luck worried me.
That traffic light changing on me when I was late to a meeting?
It was a sign—I hadn't worried enough. It showed that God or
whoever was running the universe was intent on me failing. If,
in a similar situation, I made all the lights? Well, then destiny
was back on my side.

So, yeah, I had some issues when it came to processing
stress. But I would add a corollary to the advice from that psychologist. If you process stress poorly, you're better off if you
have less of it.

The changes in my life after winning a seat in the Washington State Senate at age twenty-five greatly reduced the stress in my life, and that helped. My life, as I viewed it, was on track. I had far greater confidence and could relax more. It gave me a decent fifteen-year run. My career progressed nicely, leading me to winning a seat in Congress and managing to get reelected every two years after that without much difficulty. I got married, had two kids, and was pretty lucky on both fronts. I had a good marriage, and our children were healthy and developing well. I felt successful, and that mattered to me. It gave me confidence.

Despite this period of happiness and prosperity, warning signs had emerged.

Just under five months after my election victory in November of 1990 a bout of severe depression hit me. It was March of the following year, a week or so after I had my wisdom teeth removed. Interestingly, my three seemingly out-of-the-blue attacks of anxiety or depression have all started in the month of March. My father died in March of 1985, when I was nineteen. And, yes, over the years, therapists have poked around this fact to no particular conclusion.

This wave of depression and occasional anxiety also made no sense to me at the time. I had arrived. I was happy. Life was good. So, what the hell? But for several months I couldn't shake it. I was in a state of deep depression.

It did, as would happen again years later, manifest itself in that one particular fear—the inevitability of my own death. I hadn't really given that much thought prior to this time, which prompted my best friend, someone I had known since we met in the first grade, to offer the idea that maybe I figured I finally had something to lose. He was familiar with the dark outlook of my teenage years and the joy I felt after winning my election.

I would have put it somewhat differently. I was obsessed with succeeding in life. I had to vanquish whatever challenges or obstacles stood in the way of that success. I possessed an odd optimism about this. I honestly believed God or fate or whoever had a plan for me. I would find a way. If I worked hard enough, thought long enough, I would find a way to win. Hell, a poll taken by the Senate Democratic Campaign Committee in June 1990 showed me down 61–12 to my opponent, but in the end, I found a way to win. What obstacle could I not overcome? Yeah, well, that would be death. Time waits for no person, right?

But the depression didn't come from this thought. It just hit me, and then I started thinking about it. And it passed. By July of that year, it disappeared completely, without me seeking help or treatment.

Stress also entered my life during this fifteen-year period. My 1994 reelection campaign pushed me to the edge of endurance. It was not a good year to be a Democrat, and I faced the very real possibility of my seemingly promising career going off a cliff in an embarrassing loss to a guy I considered to be little more than a charlatan and a fool. I stressed my way through it. Did the work and worried, worried, worried. I survived. My 1996 run for Congress presented similar challenges. But I stuck to the plan. Work, work, work. Think, think, think. Worry, worry, worry. Again, I succeeded.

Then came the children. I love my children dearly and feel truly blessed to have both of them in my life. They are, as I write this, now entering adulthood, and I have strong relationships with both of them. I can honestly say that for all the professional success I have had, some of the greatest joy of my life has come from our shared experiences as a family.

Chris Matthews, the onetime TV host and political journalist, used to like to say that in Washington, DC, when listening to a political speaker, best to ignore everything before the "but . . ."

So, please don't ignore everything before the "but. . . ." It is heartfelt and sincere. But . . .

I had no experience with children. Literally none. For the first thirty-five years of my life, I was that guy visiting friends with a baby who tried to not even think about holding the kid, and if I did? Think Donald Trump trying to figure out what to do with that Bible in front of St. John's Church during the George Floyd protests. Not a pretty picture.

I always wanted to be married and truly love being married. I never gave children much thought. My wife is the oldest of five children, with a mother who has taught small children all her life. When I proposed, I knew we would have children, and I accepted that. Otherwise, I still didn't give it much thought.

Did the stress I felt during my 1994 reelection campaign compare to the stress I felt during the time my children were babies? Not even close. I like to say that I spent the first year of my first child's life trying to figure out how to talk my wife out of having a second child. I did, as with some of those other stressful experiences that came before, figure it out enough to get comfortable and welcome that second child into our home. But it wasn't easy.

I crave order in my life, another defense against stress and anxiety. I make to-do lists, try to plan things out so I know what to expect, all in an effort to give me the illusion of control in an uncertain world. And I work hard to keep the peace with people in my immediate surroundings. Again, disorder triggers stress for me. Upset people cause disorder.

Babies defy these efforts. They rarely stick to schedules or preset plans. They get upset. A lot. They cry. A lot. Often without clear evidence of why. I know, I know. They're either hungry or they're tired. Yeah, right. Sometimes they're just upset; I get that. It just stressed me out to not have an immediate idea of how to address the concerns of my children.

And talk about responsibility. Babies literally rely on their parents to keep them alive from one day to the next. Suddenly, I was that parent. A character in the Michael Connelly novel *A Darkness More Than Night* summed it up like this when asked how he felt about being a new father. "It's like having a gun to your head all the time. Because I know, if anything happens to her, anything, then my life is over."

Okay, I'm not that dark in my outlook, but I clearly felt the pressure to keep both of my children breathing. Failure may not have been an option, but I knew enough to know it was a terrifying possibility.

I also rely a great deal on reason and logic. I actually have done quite well dealing with my children as teenagers. I have an outsized amount of confidence in my ability to persuade people of things. I make a living doing that, and I have studied the art for a very long time. I love a challenge in this regard. People look at the world in an infinite number of different ways, but with patience and keen powers of listening and observation, one can learn how to deal with most anybody. Even teenagers.

I would say that nobody on God's green earth can use reason and logic with a baby. They don't speak and have limited powers of understanding. But I have seen my mother-in-law somehow manage to do it, so I know it's just something I never figured out how to do myself. Skipping any further details, the experience stressed me out.

By March of 2005, I was flying back and forth from DC most weeks, rushing through an abbreviated workweek and desperately hoping the House would end votes on Thursday or Friday in time for me to make the mad dash out to Dulles Airport to catch the nonstop flight home so I didn't have to make the agonizing decision to take a flight out of National, connecting through Chicago (something always goes wrong at O'Hare), hopefully arriving home in time to offer some—admittedly not as helpful as it could have been—relief to my wife in caring for our children, then doing whatever meetings I had to do with my constituents before Monday or Tuesday when I had to get back on the plane to head to DC, arriving, hopefully, in time to rush to the House floor to make that evening's votes, and oh, by the way, sleeping on an Aerobed in my office that I had to blow up every night and deflate every morning so I could stuff it in a closet because, with two children, paying for a place in DC stretched our budget and, at the end of the day, I'm kind of a minimalist when it comes to living quarters anyway so why pay for an apartment that I would just have to clean and maintain when I wouldn't even be in it for more than about a third of the year and slowly starting to worry about the direction of my career now that I had spent over eight years in the minority party with nowhere near the political power I wanted and my early endorsement and support for John Kerry's presidential run having not panned out when he wound up losing, and still dealing with severe back pain that had hit six years earlier and that I hadn't ever quite figured out.

I snapped. Why exactly, the above notwithstanding, I couldn't say. How did I go from the rising and falling waves of stress to the constant inescapable crush of anxiety? No safe place existed anymore. The anxiety followed me everywhere. I couldn't stress my way through one of my children being ill and then relax on the flight to DC or at a ballgame with a friend. The anxiety was my constant shadow.

I needed help.

CHAPTER 4
My First Psychiatrist
MARCH 2005

n times of stress, I usually write out lists in an effort to organize my thoughts and develop a game plan. Most of the time, the simple act of writing focuses me and enables me to calm down. Faced with obstacles to whatever goal I am trying to achieve, I think through the problem and in that process find a path to success. I understand—and to some degree, even back then, understood—that life offers few guarantees. Just give me a chance, show me steps that I can take to make success more likely, and let me believe I have a path.

I saw no path to relief from my anxiety in March of 2005. The effects of the anxiety itself were bad enough—constant, existential fear coursing through my body, an almost complete inability to sleep, so stressed that I could only just barely force myself to eat. But more than anything, I had no idea whatsoever how this had happened or what I could do about it. I felt like I was stumbling around in absolute darkness, completely unable to see, with something or somebody whacking me in the head with a blunt object every few seconds—blows I never saw coming.

I decided to call my doctor back in DC, figuring I had to try something, even though I couldn't really see a path between the doctor who gave me an annual physical and treating my anxiety. I didn't know any psychiatrists at the time and had a built-in skepticism about their efficacy. I pictured in my mind a headline from the satirical newspaper the *Onion* I'd seen a few years prior: "Psychiatrist Actually Cures Someone."

I explained my symptoms, and my doctor recommended that I speak with a Navy psychiatrist who worked at the US Naval Medical Center in Bethesda, Maryland. I could not see him in person because my schedule had me back home in Washington State for the week, so my doctor set a time for me to speak to the psychiatrist on the phone.

"What seems to be the problem?" he asked, quickly getting to the point. I had managed to consider this question prior to the call, to try to figure out how to explain it in a way that would at least offer some clarity.

I walked through the above-described symptoms and then said, "It feels like a switch has been flipped in my mind, causing me to suddenly see almost everything as a mortal threat."

"What do you mean by everything?"

"I don't know. Everything. Everything I hear or see. Or think about. For some reason it terrifies me." He hesitated, apparently waiting for something more specific. "Okay," I added. "Last night, watching some pointless TV show with my family, and there's this ten-year-old girl in the show. I'm trying to care about whatever problem it is she is facing, but my mind tells me, *What's the point? She's going to die at some point like everybody else*. And the thought terrified me. Like I said, suddenly every thought I have, everything I see, almost literally everything I experience in the world around me is causing this sense of terror."

"That's a perfectly natural reaction," he assured me. "Most people have to deal with this at some point in their lives. How to handle the inevitability of death."

"But it's not like I'm just now becoming aware of it. Why am I suddenly freaking out?"

He didn't have an immediate answer for this and kept asking me for details about what was going on in my life, trying to tease out what had happened to me to trigger my extreme anxiety.

"That's just it," I said in frustration. "I have no idea. Nothing has really changed that much from ten days ago when I wasn't in this state of absolute, constant panic."

"Okay," he said eventually, "let's do this. Find a time for you to come see me so we can talk through it. When will you be in DC next?"

Again, this simple question caused my anxiety to spike. I could barely stand the thought of being this way for one more hour, much less the week that would pass before I could see him. And when I saw him, then what? What could he possibly have to say that would change my outlook on all this and calm me down? I still couldn't see a path.

"I can prescribe some medication to help in the short term," he said, after I had explained the first part of my concerns.

I lacked trust in this suggestion as well. My experience in the world of drugs or, if you prefer, medication to that point in my life consisted of only three things—alcohol, an aversion to pain medication, and the fruitless use of various drugs a few years earlier in an attempt to deal with a bad digestive system.

I drank my first beer at age fifteen and consumed a reasonably steady amount of alcohol for ten years after that. Why? I don't have a great explanation for that. I didn't have much parental supervision at that point in my life. I was, as I've described, frustrated with life and looking for an escape from that frustration, and, more than anything, my friends and I were bored teenagers growing up in a working-class suburb where there wasn't much to do. So, we drank. And we stole toilet paper wherever we could find it to deposit in ever more creative ways on the houses of our other friends.

I was lucky. My genes and my environment, for whatever reason, did not incline me toward addiction. I stopped drinking to excess shortly after my twenty-fifth birthday. Most of the time, one does survive being young and stupid.

Pain medication worried me, and I resisted taking it. My doctor and I argued this point on and off for a while as I struggled to deal with knee and back pain. "I can deal with pain," I would tell him. "I don't trust the pain relievers."

"Okay," he reasoned. "Don't think of it as pain medication. Think of it as an anti-inflammatory."

But my problem was twofold. First, pain relievers mask pain, and if I use my body in a way that would normally cause pain, but I don't feel it, I might be doing more damage to myself. Second, I liked to use pain relievers only when absolutely necessary because I feared becoming tolerant to their palliative effects and then not being able to get the relief when I truly needed it. If I had a bad headache, for example, I took pain medication. I couldn't function with a bad headache.

My doctor assured me you do not develop a tolerance from taking ibuprofen or acetaminophen. I still don't believe that, and I am strongly of the opinion that most doctors way underestimate how quickly we humans can develop this type of tolerance for a variety of drugs.

The reflux drugs I took to treat what was diagnosed to me as a very bad heartburn problem never helped. They created more problems in my digestive system. Now, admittedly, as I learned about my anxiety issues, it is more than possible that the symptoms I was experiencing that seemed like heartburn/digestive issues might have had a mental component, but I didn't realize that at this point. I just knew that the drugs seemed to not quite work as advertised.

Desperate, I put aside all of these concerns and picked up the prescription the psychiatrist phoned in to my local pharmacy. The pills were clonazepam—0.5 milligram pills, ten of them in this prescription. I picked them up with a sense of shame more in line with somebody trying to score heroin in a back alley. What if the pharmacist recognized me? He knew what these pills were for. I'd be outed as a mental patient, and I didn't want that label. I also, without giving the matter much thought, concluded my career would be over. Voters, I figured, wouldn't want to be represented by somebody with a debilitating mental illness.

Then I took one. Forty-five minutes later? Oh. My. God. It was awesome. My anxiety melted away like an ice cube on a hot summer day. Gone. Like it was never there. I was myself again. I could think clearly. Enjoy life. It was unbelievable. I wasn't high. It wasn't like the euphoria that drinking had sometimes brought me. It just made me feel like I used to feel.

I maintained my concerns about tolerance, so over the next couple of months, I used the clonazepam sparingly, only taking one pill every two or three days. I tried to hold out until I couldn't take the anxiety anymore. This approach introduced me to another concept in regard to taking medication that, though I had not previously experienced it, would become a not-insignificant challenge in my overall healthcare battle in the years to come— withdrawals.

I started seeing the psychiatrist out at Bethesda once a week after I returned to DC. I told only my chief of staff. We had to keep it as secret as possible. Again, I figured that we couldn't have people thinking a member of Congress had misplaced his marbles. I drove myself out to Bethesda for the appointments, sneaking out like I was on some kind of classified spy mission.

"You don't have to do anything," my psychiatrist said calmly. "Thinking that you do just puts more pressure on you. We just need to talk and better understand your life."

We sat in a small office with white walls on the eighth floor of the medical center. He sat behind a small wood desk, me in a simple armchair in front of him. Diplomas dotted the wall to my left, but I hadn't bothered to look at them closely enough to track his educational history.

"I just don't understand that," I responded. "I have to do

something. Isn't that the point? If I wasn't doing something wrong, I wouldn't be overwhelmed with anxiety."

"You can't look at it that way."

And yet I do, I thought but didn't say. "What about the meditation you have me doing?" I asked instead. "Isn't that 'doing something'?"

He smiled broadly. He looked to be about fifty years old, stocky, with a completely bald head. "Just the opposite. Meditation is about not doing something."

I had started this practice shortly after our first session together two weeks earlier. The peace prayer of Saint Francis of Assisi. I got up every morning now and spent twenty minutes reciting it over and over again from memory.

"Well, I guess I'm not, not doing it right because it doesn't seem to be working. I just feel like I have to get my spirituality right."

He shook his head slightly and repeated, "You don't have to do anything."

I had asked him during my first visit what religion he was. "Christian," he had responded. "We'd all be in a lot of trouble if God didn't exist." This statement from him had marinated around in my brain uncomfortably. *And would you mind offering me some absolute proof of that?* I thought. I had asked because of the whole death thing. If God absolutely existed—and I did believe He did, just not without a hint or two of doubt—and I had a soul—you know, life after death and all that, then death wouldn't be worth fearing as much. I had always considered myself a Christian, went to a Jesuit college, but had never attended church. So maybe I needed to start. This was what I meant by getting my spirituality right.

"I still can't get to sleep at night," I said, again trying to get the focus of our conversation on what I needed to do. "I start to drift off and then I jerk back awake. Heart pounding, muscles tense, stomach in knots. It's like my body is saying, what the hell are you doing? We can't go to sleep. We haven't solved the problem yet."

"What problem?" he asked.

"I don't know. That's the whole point."

"What do you think it is?"

I had developed a healthy dislike for the Socratic method during my time in law school. I kept thinking, *Wouldn't it be a whole lot easier if you just told us the answer? You obviously know and then we would know, too. Isn't that the goal?* I liked the approach even less coming from my psychiatrist.

I sat searching for an answer to his question, but nothing came to mind. I was so tired, my mind a jumbled mess, struggling to settle on any one concrete thought at a time.

"Why are you so reluctant to tell me about your childhood?" he asked when I offered no response to his previous question.

I let out a long, slow breath. "I'm not. I don't mind talking about it. I just don't see the point. My anxiety is here, now. Not in the past."

"I think it will help."

I leaned back in my chair and looked to the left at his diplomas. Naval Academy undergrad, not surprising. Johns Hopkins medical school. So, the guy wasn't a moron. *Reassuring*, I thought.

"Okay. Fine. Here's the story.

"I grew up in SeaTac, Washington. Well, technically I was

born in Washington, DC, but I was adopted. My parents flew to DC to get me. I spent the first five years of my life in a single-wide trailer in a community appropriately named Trailer Town. We then moved to a 1,000-square-foot rambler in the same town a couple of miles away. My father was a ramp serviceman, a baggage handler for United Airlines at the airport. That's why we lived in SeaTac. My mother raised my two-years-older brother, me, and six years after I arrived, my younger brother. She did go back to work when I was a teenager, delivering newspapers on a motor paper route.

"I didn't know I was adopted until I was twenty-six years old. I guess they were supposed to tell me but never did. I got a letter after both my parents had died. The woman I grew up thinking was my aunt, my father's youngest sister, was actually my mother. She lived in DC. That's why I was born there. She sent me the letter."

"Fascinating," he said, briefly interrupting my story.

"Okay. My father died when he was nineteen. I was off at college in New York when he had a massive stroke. I got home, and five days later he had another massive stroke in the hospital and died."

"Fascinating," he said again with a look of wonder on his face. He had begun looking at me like I was some kind of exotic zoo animal.

"My mother died," I continued, "the night before I won my election to the state Senate, also of a stroke. She suffered it as she was working her paper route Sunday morning. It left her brain-dead, and she died a day and a half later. Nine months after she passed, I got the letter. My biological mother lived in Florida by that point and was married with two kids of her own.

"My older brother was a nightmare. He wasn't adopted, and neither was my younger brother. My older brother pulled a knife on me once. Beat me up a couple of other times and stole from me and everyone else in the family. Series of arrests as a teenager. Dropped out of high school. Joined the Army. Dropped out of that as well. More arrests and right now I couldn't say for sure if he is even alive. My younger brother seems okay. Got arrested for selling pot a few years back, but he's a good kid. It was more of a business deal for him.

"I never met my biological father. Apparently, he wanted nothing to do with me or my aunt, uh, mother, from the moment he found out she was pregnant. I did find him. Right after I learned I was adopted. Retired. Living, ironically, in Falls Church, Virginia, but I never saw the point in meeting him. I guess I drive by his neighborhood twice a week now as I head out to Dulles, on weeks when I'm coming and going from DC.

"If I feel guilty about anything, it's that I didn't do more to help my mother after my father died. We just never seemed to be that close, and I didn't know what to do. And I was busy. Trying to turn my life around. Be who I was supposed to be. I didn't even know that, when she died, she didn't have health insurance. Shocked me when the hospital gave me the bill."

"Fascinating," my psychiatrist said one more time. "Freud would have loved you. You think you killed your father."

"What? No."

"You said your father died when he was nineteen."

"What? No. He died when *I* was nineteen. Look, I'm beyond

exhausted here. No sleep, stressed out of my mind. It just came out the wrong way."

"They call them Freudian slips for a reason."

"Look," I said, finally finding a degree of focus. "I don't think I killed my father. If anything drove him to an early grave, that would be my older brother and all of his issues. If anything, I think I killed my mother. Like I said, I didn't help her that much after my father died."

He just nodded with a knowing look on his face. What this meant, I couldn't begin to guess and never did figure out.

CHAPTER 5

The Storm Passes and a New Life Plan Emerges

These discussions went on for six weeks, to no helpful conclusion. Maybe the guy knew what he was doing, and I just couldn't figure it out, but it didn't seem to be helping me. I finally stopped taking the clonazepam in early June, fought my way through the relatively minor withdrawal symptoms—mild increase in anxiety and inability to sleep—and started to calm down. I stopped seeing the psychiatrist. I started going to church and kept meditating. I slowly got back to normal without ever really understanding why, or why the anxiety had hit in the first place.

In November, I went on a congressional trip to visit our troops in Iraq. A trip to a war zone is not for the faint of heart, even with the security that comes with us, but I was fine, not even a hint of the anxiety that had so knocked me back earlier in the year. Scars remained, however. I remembered the anxiety vividly. I didn't want it to return. What changes could I make to my life to best help ensure it didn't?

Physical pain, for much of my life, had caused me to change certain activities. My right knee hurt after my surgery in high school. I learned that I could stay active—run, play basketball, and so on—but I had to be careful. Climbing stairs too much caused pain over time so I tried to avoid that and tried to put more weight on my left leg when I couldn't avoid it. Eventually, running caused my right knee to swell, so I downshifted to walking fast and up hills because, for some reason, walking up hills did not hurt my knee the way climbing stairs did. I responded to the onset of my back pain in a variety of ways; most notably I learned it hurt if I sat for too long without back support, so I avoided that. I later learned the error of my ways in this regard, but at the time I simply concluded I needed to apply the same logic to the threat my anxiety presented.

My biggest conclusion was that I had simply tried to do too much. I got moving too fast, and, like a car running at top speed for too long, I blew out my engine—or in my case, me not actually being a car, my brain. I needed to find a way to slow down and give my brain some rest.

My children, at this point ages six and three, had become more manageable, so that helped. I viewed meditation and going to church as efforts at allowing my brain to relax in a more spiritual realm, though at times these activities felt like just two more things my overly taxed mind had to fit into the schedule. I liked to joke, "I'm stressed out because I'm worried about finding time to meditate." I knew, however, that these things merely represented working around the edges of my I-got-going-too-fast problem. My job was the core of the issue. I had to live in two places, log over 100,000 miles in the air each year, and juggle an endless array of people and issues every day in order to do that job. I had always believed that that force in the universe I keep referencing wanted me to achieve at a very high level in my chosen profession of politics, and to be, if not perfect, then close to it. Now, my anxiety attack led me to believe the universe might be sending a different message.

I decided my campaign for reelection to Congress in 2006 would be my last. I had no meaningful opposition that year, so winning posed no challenge. I still believed politics, public service, and public policy to be my calling, so I settled on running for a local office in 2008, one that wouldn't require me to live in two places or spend anywhere near as much time on an airplane.

Logical holes could easily be poked into this plan. I would still have to mount a campaign with all the pressure inherent in that effort. I could easily lose. Perhaps being the executive of a medium-sized county would prove to be more of a challenge, even if it enabled me to have a short commute back to my own home every night. But I was making my decision based mostly on fear. This was my life. That life, as a member of Congress, led me to a very painful place. Ergo, I had to change that life. I had thought that life was the one for me and fought hard to make it possible, but obviously I had been wrong.

I got a little schizophrenic on this issue in the months that followed—committed to my new life plan, but always with doubts lurking not far from the surface of this plan. I mean, was I wrong about what I was supposed to do with my life? Really? Could that be possible? I loved my life. Loved the memories of how that life had been built. Far from wishing it had been easier, I had always enjoyed the memories of the struggle and the setbacks, almost as much as the successes. It proved something to me about myself. I could take a punch and fight my way through tough circumstances. How could the universe now require me to walk away from it?

Faced with near certain defeat in my first state Senate race, I let my campaign manager talk me into propping up that campaign by borrowing $2,500 on my only credit card, which I had never before allowed to accumulate even one penny of interest. "We'll find another way to win," he said in June, five months from the election, with great confidence and absolutely no idea how that would happen. I had just told him that the five groups I had been counting on donating around $150,000 to my campaign had decided to give nothing. One of them endorsed my Republican opponent.

We found another way to win. I loved that process. I went for a run in my neighborhood the night the election board declared the results of my election official. I crested a hill along the way and thought to myself, *If anybody on the face of God's green earth has ever felt this good in their life, I can't imagine it.*

Two years later, I traveled around our state, recruiting Democratic candidates for the Senate seats that were up that year (they have four-year terms with roughly half of them up each two-year cycle) and working to help elect enough Democrats for our party to retake the majority. We did: 28–21. My leadership team named me chair of the Senate Law and Justice Committee (Judiciary basically, under a different name). I was twenty-seven and running one of the most important committees in the Senate. I took the job, both as a senator and as chairman, very seriously. I worked hard and enjoyed the challenge, even if I overstressed about aspects of it. I felt like I was making a difference doing what I was supposed to be doing.

My own reelection campaign in 1994 presented challenges, as I have described, but I learned from them. I made mistakes. I got angry and frustrated, which were very unhelpful emotions and ones I realized came to me out of proportion to what the circumstances warranted. Nevertheless, I learned, and I survived.

Less than a year after that reelection, I decided to run for Congress—July 3, 1995, to be exact. I remember the date because I was sitting in a movie theater with two of my friends watching *Pulp Fiction* when this thought literally entered my head: *I'm supposed to run for Congress.*

I had an odd mental block on the issue prior to that moment. I wanted a full-time job as an elected official, that much I knew. I loved being a state senator, but it was part-time. I got married the year before, and my wife was in law school. I needed greater stability. I thought about running for attorney general, even secretary of state, but neither worked in the 1996 election for varying reasons. One would assume that a national legislative office would have long been on my radar, but I had decided, back in my teenage years as I dreamed of a career in politics, that Congress made no sense. It was in DC, 2,500 miles across the country. That didn't work. I'd work my way up to governor and go from there.

Literally, this "plan," created from a child's daydream, led me to offer this response to the Democratic Congressional Campaign Committee in April of 1995, when they asked me to consider running for the seat in Washington's Ninth District: "Nope. Not interested." I held that position right up until that July 3 afternoon when, for some reason, that mental block finally disappeared.

Campaigns aside, I loved the job. I always say that, whatever popular opinion may believe, politics, at its best, is about bringing diverse people with widely differing opinions together and finding a way to bridge those differences and solve problems— to make our community safer, more prosperous and just, and a better place to live for all of us. I have hundreds of stories of when my staff and I have been able to do that, even those times when it seemed highly unlikely to occur. I love doing that and loved doing it back in 2006 when I decided to walk away from Congress.

My point is that I had passionately believed for almost my entire adult life that I was doing what I was supposed to be doing. But in 2006, I didn't want to believe that anymore because if I believed that, if I believed that I was destined to accumulate as much political power as possible in order to help people, then I had failed. I had been too weak to do what I was supposed to do. So, I attempted to convince myself that I was really supposed to do something else now.

I only told a few of my most senior advisers of this plan to not run for Congress in 2008, and they, for their part, attempted to humor me. They didn't say what I suspected they thought, namely, "Are you insane? You love being in Congress. You're building seniority, and you're still young enough to do something with it. You'd give that up for some rinky-dink local government job where you will work on filling potholes and hiring a new ombudsman?" Instead, they went with "If that's what you think is best."

They did, however, also point out that Democrats had a decent shot to win back the majority in 2006. I should, they argued, position myself to chair a subcommittee on the House Armed Services Committee, to be ready if we took the majority. They believed I would be in line to chair the Terrorism and Unconventional Threats Subcommittee with jurisdiction over, among other things, the Special Operations Command (SOCOM). I more or less shrugged off the suggestion. I didn't want to think about the possibility of more power and more responsibility coming my way. I thought I couldn't handle it anyway.

The thing I feared was the return of my fear, to paraphrase FDR. I was not experiencing anxiety anymore. I was just still spooked by the possibility of its return. I could still recall that all-consuming feeling of terror that had invaded my entire being—knots in my stomach constantly, unable to sleep, struggling to eat, with all of those symptoms spiking even higher with everything I experienced in my life.

Absent this fear, just like in the state Senate in 1992, I would have been out there running around the country, trying to support our candidates in an effort to get that majority back.

This time, I sat out the battle. I also harbored doubts Democrats would, in fact, win. We had been flailing about for twelve years and six election cycles without success. Why would that change now?

I did know that Congressman Rahm Emanuel had taken over the campaign arm of our caucus and realized Rahm had a, shall we say, more focused and aggressive approach to campaigning than his predecessors in the job. I had often thought of myself in this mold—one who understood that all the lofty policy ideas in the world go nowhere if you don't do the work and fight aggressively on the campaign trail. Then I met Rahm. He took this attitude to a whole other level. A lobbyist friend of mine put it this way, "Rahm's a stone-cold killer. He plays to win." And, in 2006, he and Nancy Pelosi, our minority leader and soon to be Speaker of the House, won, leading the Democrats back into power in the House.

This rattled me a little. Part of my argument to my staff for leaving had been the reality of suffering through over a decade in the minority party. That doesn't change anything, I rationalized. I'm still mid-tier in seniority. I won't have any real power. I recognized the schizophrenia here. I had decided to leave because I was afraid I couldn't handle the responsibility of being a member of Congress while at the same time arguing I was leaving because I didn't have more responsibility. Again, I was acting out of fear—fear I didn't really understand.

Yes, I remembered my staff muttering about me chairing a subcommittee, but I had dismissed that as my staff letting their enthusiasm outpace their math skills. I was tenth in seniority on the House Armed Services Committee. The committee would have one very powerful chair and six reasonably powerful sub-committee chairs. That's seven. I was tenth. Okay, one of those nine Democrats ahead of me would be the chair of the Budget Committee and the rules prohibited any member from chairing more than one committee, but that only got us up to eight.

I could not, however, ignore the energy and enthusiasm buzzing through my fellow Democrats that November as we assembled in Washington, DC, to begin the process of electing our leadership team and committee chairs, and then appointing members to committees and other positions. We were dividing up the spoils of victory, if you will. It reminded me of the rush I felt back in 1992 when the incoming state Senate majority leader called me and told me I would chair Law and Justice.

Then the newly selected incoming chair of the House Armed Services Committee decided to add a seventh subcommittee, something he and the committee staff had, unbeknownst to me, been planning to do as they anticipated our return to power. Okay, that's nine. I'm still tenth.

I still don't know why Nancy Pelosi decided to pick Silvester Reyes to chair the Intelligence Committee that year. Since that time, I have developed a close working relationship with Speaker Pelosi, but it has never occurred to me to ask her about this. Silver, as everybody called him, was one of those Democratic members ahead of me in seniority on the Armed Services Committee.

That made it ten.

"The Terrorism Subcommittee is yours if you want it," my chief of staff told me. "And hey, I just met this Navy SEAL who served multiple tours in Iraq and Afghanistan. He's the new SO-COM liaison to the House. He's excited to have you as chair and wants to take you all over the world and show you what the Special Ops guys do. Also, he has a trip at the end of this week down to Virginia Beach. Several SOF groups are based down there. Anyway, the subcommittee's yours if you want it."

There's a scene in the movie *Old School* where Will Ferrell's character, Frank, is asked to take a hit from a beer bong. He's at a crowded, wild, and loud fraternity party. He's recently married and has promised his wife that his drinking and partying days are behind him. He winds up at the party because of the central premise of the movie, an admittedly preposterous plotline where Frank's friend Mitch, despite being, like Frank, in his early thirties and long out of college, rents a house close to the local college campus and is talked into trying to start his own fraternity at this house. The party, featuring live music from Snoop Dog, launches the fraternity.

Frank has promised his wife he won't drink at the launch party. He grabs a couple of sodas and is working his way through the crowded house toward the backyard when a few students ask him to take the beer bong hit. He declines and goes on to explain that he has a busy day tomorrow.

One of the students frowns and asks, "Busy day? Doing what?"

"Actually, it's kind of a nice little Saturday," Frank answers. "We're going to Home Depot. Get some wallpaper. And some flooring. Then maybe Bed, Bath and Beyond. But I don't know. Don't know if we'll have time."

The students snort with laughter, mocking Frank's chosen way to spend a Saturday.

"You know what," Frank says, clearly offended. "Give me that thing. I'll do one."

He downs the beer in a few seconds, and with a look of pure enjoyment says, "Hit it up again. It's just so good. Once it hits your lips, it's just so good."

It's very difficult to stop doing something when you have grown accustomed to doing that thing, when it becomes what people expect of you. It's even harder when a pretty big part of you really enjoys doing that thing. Democrats getting the majority back or not, subcommittee chair or no subcommittee chair, I seriously doubt that, at the end of the day, I would have pulled the trigger and left Congress in 2008.

CHAPTER 6
A Good Six-Year Run

M y decision not to leave Congress led to an amazing six-year run in my life. I loved chairing that subcommittee. I loved going to Iraq, Afghanistan, huge chunks of Africa, the Middle East, Europe, and Asia and visiting our Special Forces, learning more about how they operate, and meeting a diverse group of fascinating people all over the globe. Back home in the United States, I toured bases and training sites all over the country. I also endorsed Barack Obama very early in his campaign for president and, when he won, was able to develop a strong working relationship with many key players in his administration. Speaker Pelosi appointed me to the Intelligence Committee after

the 2008 election cycle, which, combined with my seat on Armed
Services, gave me a great background on a wide range of interesting
national security issues.

One of my trips to Afghanistan during this time period
included a ride in a Blackhawk helicopter out to a US-run firebase in Paktika Province, right on the edge of the border with
Pakistan. It was a garrison of a few dozen Special Forces troops
working with Afghan partners to secure the area from Taliban
insurgents. Bad weather grounded the helicopter for seven
hours and extended my stay at the firebase well into the night.

The Special Forces soldiers decided to practice some mortar fire that night, firing some dummy rounds into the empty
hills surrounding the base. I watched as they dropped the shells
down the short tube and then ducked away as the shells rock-
eted out and into the sky. A few other civilians, staff, and State
Department people had joined me on the trip, and the soldiers
started asking if they wanted to drop a round. A couple did,
most declined, and the soldiers would ask those who took a
pass, "What? Are you scared?"

They looked at me and I shook my head before they could
even ask. "Yes," I said. "I'm scared. I don't want to kill all of you,
and I certainly don't want to kill myself."

But I wasn't really scared in the truest sense of the word. At
that point in my life, I knew what scared was. This wasn't that.
It was a rational concern about doing something stupid and the
potential consequences. It was one of many signs, to me, that I
had put my demon back safely in its box.

That same night I overheard a few of the Special Forces soldiers talking as the mortar practice continued. One of them had

apparently been at Blackhawk Down in Somalia the previous decade, where US troops had been ambushed and lost eighteen members of their team. He described what it felt like to get hit by a .50-caliber round. He told the story casually, like others might describe a tough day at work, but I will always remember his closing line.

"Whoever dies with the most stories wins. And I'm already a winner."

I liked that life philosophy. I wanted a life full of interesting and challenging experiences with the caveat that I wasn't willing to go as far as the guys around me that night. I didn't ever want to be able to say from experience what it felt like to be hit by a round of any caliber.

I thought I had that life at that point—challenging and interesting with a relatively low and easily manageable risk of premature catastrophic failure.

My family life also thrived. My wife and I enjoyed watching our children grow, seeing the development in each of their own unique personalities. We traveled with them a lot around the United States. We went to DC every summer and added side trips to Boston, New York, Philadelphia, Maine, Charleston, Williamsburg—showing our children the East Coast and some of our nation's history. We went to Disneyland three times. We were active and enjoyed our lives, even if it wasn't always perfect. The kids got sick but never seriously. We had arguments and difficulties. My children quickly coined the phrase, "It's not a vacation until Mom says we're never going on a vacation again."

But I found it all manageable, and the reality of how well my life seemed to be going once again gave me the confidence of feeling comfortable and secure in my place in the world.

My first trip to Africa is a good example of my outlook. I led a congressional delegation (CODEL) of six members of Congress, several spouses, and a half dozen staff. We visited seven countries in ten days.

One leg of the journey involved taking a United Nations helicopter from Kigali, Rwanda, into the eastern part of the Democratic Republic of the Congo. We landed in Kigali and then left our Department of Defense C-40 there, taking a short drive to another part of the airport to board the helicopter. We all arrived at the helicopter, did a double take, and then looked at one another, like *we are going to die.* It was a Soviet-era Russian helicopter that looked like it might just fall apart where it sat. My Navy SEAL liaison friend was staffing the trip, and he just laughed. "Come on. It's fine." He and I had been a lot of places in a lot of marginal situations at this point, and I trusted him implicitly. I did, however, like to point out to him that while he was trained and relatively used to life-or-death combat situations, I was very much not. But, because of that trust, I quickly joined in his laughter and waved everybody onto the helicopter. He always assured me that the last thing he wanted to do was kill off a member of Congress. It would look bad on his record.

Then we met the pilot—an equally old and creaky-looking Russian. I felt reasonably confident he wasn't actually drunk at that moment but absolutely confident he probably was much of the time. His preflight instructions included his helpful hint, also from a bygone era, that if anything went wrong, the ladies on our trip should look to the men to protect them. Congress-woman Gabby Giffords was one of the members of Congress on the trip. She, as the world would soon learn, is utterly fearless. She looked like she wanted to gouge his eyeballs out. I leaned over to her and said, "Gabby, if you kill this guy, who's going to get us into the DRC?"

And that was how I looked at the entire experience. It was enormously entertaining. A few years prior I had been afraid of pretty much everything. Now, this whole situation struck me as amusing. I was fairly certain we wouldn't die and loved having the opportunity to be around so many interesting people in such a fascinating part of the world. And I was, more or less, in charge. It was my trip. How crazy was that?

It wasn't just amusing, however. I also enjoyed the parts of it that were very serious. The parts that involved figuring out how we might in some small way help people who faced terri-fying situations—violent conflict, famine, being displaced from their homes, the seemingly relentless pain and suffering that inflicted that part of the world and so many others.

The eastern DRC suffered from the spillover from the previ-ous decade's genocidal conflict in Rwanda and the long-running civil war that Uganda had gone through during that time frame, as well as their own internal struggles. We visited one of many refugee camps in the region during our trip. It was for internally displaced persons, people uprooted from their homes when one violent group or another poured into their town and tried to take control, usually from some other violent group that had only recently wrested control from somebody else. It was a mess, and the refugee camps had issues of their own—the biggest one being the culture that had settled into this lawlessness of rape as just a part of life.

The UN people who had helped set up the refugee camp asked if a couple of the members of Congress would be willing to visit with some of the rape victims. Gabby volunteered immediately and then, almost as quickly, volunteered me to join her. I was in charge, after all. I was willing to do this but not eager by any means. I liked helping people, but how on earth could I help in this situation? What would we say?

Gabby and I speaking to the women, of course, wasn't the point. The point was listening, trying in some small way to let these women know that they weren't alone.

The other thing we could do, we learned as we listened to these women tell their stories through a translator, was to go and meet with the men living in the camp who served as a kind of ad hoc leadership of the community. We could at least try to impress upon these men that if they viewed themselves as the ones providing order for their makeshift town, they were failing miserably. The women didn't blame the men in leadership at the camp, but Gabby and I could do the math here. Women getting raped repeatedly meant a clear failure of leadership. We met with the men and did our best to make that case. I have no idea if it made a difference, but I will always be grateful to Gabby for having the courage to give us the chance to try, for helping me do the right thing in a difficult situation.

The 2010 election did not go well. I managed to survive my own reelection campaign in a year that was a historical disaster for the Democratic Party, and where we lost the majority in the House. It was a stressful time, wondering if the Republican tsunami would take me out to sea with it. But I felt like I handled it better than I used to handle such stressful situations. I worked hard and thought in great detail about the best way to survive, but the difference was that I worried less. I tried to be the happy warrior, to take on the challenge with a smile and a sense of humor to match the sense of determination instead of being angry and scared all the time. My anxiety remained an increasingly distant memory.

The loss of the majority even wound up containing a surprise bonus. Enough Democrats ahead of me in seniority on the Armed Services Committee either lost or didn't run again so that I rose to number two in seniority, behind only Silvester Reyes, who ended his four-year stint as the chair of the Intelligence Committee. He decided to run for the top spot on Armed Services. If successful, he would be the ranking member, not the chair, since Democrats were back in the minority, but for complicated reasons, being the leader of even the minority party on Armed Services carried a lot of power.

I decided to run against him for that top job, and so did the member right behind me in seniority. The 190 members of Congress who remained in the Democratic caucus after the 2010 wipeout would vote to decide which of us got the job. The first ballot split 64–64–61. I, having been one of the two tied at 64, then won the runoff, 97–86. It had been a challenging six-week campaign. I worked the phones relentlessly and talked to members around the Capitol whenever I could. The victory, once again, kept my career moving forward in a positive direction. If I could hold on to the job, I would be the chair when the Democrats regained the majority.

Joy filled my immediate environment in the aftermath of the victory. My staff and supporters imagined all we could do with our new-found position of power. Countless people congratulated me. How could all not be right with the world?

I flew home the day after the caucus vote, Congress having finally wrapped up our lame-duck session. I was eager to finally get going on my Christmas shopping and other preparations for the holiday. My flight leveled off, and the captain turned off the seat-belt sign. I got up and went to the bathroom, where I sat on the toilet seat and cried for fifteen minutes. One thought would not leave my head: I don't deserve this.

I couldn't stop thinking about my family but not the one I had at that point. The one that raised me. Why me? How did I deserve this amazing life? My parents died earlier than they should have. They died clearly unhappy with their lives. Our family had fallen apart long before they passed. I didn't fix that. I failed. And now, what? They're dead. My older brother is God knows where. Homeless? Dead already himself? And me? Everything just keeps falling into place for me. How is that fair?

My plane landed at SeaTac after the five-hour flight, and I went on about my life. The clarity and the intensity of these thoughts receded in my mind. They drifted into the background, even if they never disappeared entirely.

The shooting in Tucson, Arizona, on January 8, 2011, killed six people and devastated hundreds of people's lives. It impacted my life, but nothing in comparison to those people directly impacted. I know that. But it hit me hard. I had sat with Gabby on the House floor just one day before as we took the last votes of the week. Members, including both of us, were doing the usual dance of trying to calculate exactly when votes would end so we could decide which flight home we could catch, and then rush out for the mad dash to the airport to try to make that flight. Gabby had won a very narrow election two months earlier, having to wait for days as late absentee votes came in before being reelected by just over 4,000 votes. We talked about what she planned to do next, a run for the US Senate in 2012 being the likely answer. She even mentioned that she had just made a last-minute decision to hold a public meeting that Saturday in Tucson, something her office called "Congress on your corner."

I was with my family that Saturday morning. A woman in our community ran a hair salon out of a side room in her house, and that was where all four of us went to get our hair cut. A friend of mine, a political junkie I first met during my time in the state Senate, sent me an email. He was always sending me emails about breaking news in politics, somehow getting the information before anybody else in my immediate world. But this time what he sent me said Congresswoman Gabby Giffords had been shot while holding a public meeting with her constituents. It devastated me. The news had never been this personal. I was in shock and desperate to find out if Gabby was okay. Then the news broke that she had died—news that turned out to be wrong, but that wasn't corrected for over a half hour. It was a horrific day in so many ways for so many people.

Gabby was one of the three people to speak in favor of my candidacy for ranking member in front of the caucus. We traveled together a lot, and I honestly believe that without her, I never would have won. I am an introverted person, especially for a politician. Gabby is the polar opposite. Caucus elections are about relationships, and I didn't have that many. She did. The members of our caucus who knew me generally liked me and respected me, but a lot of them didn't know me, but they knew Gabby. And if she thought I was okay, then maybe I was, at least enough to get me those extra three votes that got me past the first round of voting.

Again, why me? Why was a woman who struck me as ten times the leader I was lying in a hospital in Tucson fighting for her life while my life just kept falling into place? You don't have to be a trained psychologist to understand the irrationality and unfairness of my thought process on all this. The family that raised me. Gabby getting shot. My life. But I couldn't completely resist that irrationality. The thoughts just kept nagging at me.

And what of this universe I kept trusting to put me on the right path? My belief in a purpose to God's creation? If there are two better people on the planet than Gabby and her husband, Mark, I haven't met them. How could the universe allow what happened to her to happen? Again, I did have some grasp on the illogic here. Bad things happen to good people every day—horrible, devastating, life-altering tragedies. Why should the fact that one of these tragedies happened to somebody I knew alter my outlook to any significant degree? I couldn't really explain that, but it, too, kept nagging at me.

These thoughts, troubling as they were, did not trigger my anxiety. I kept moving forward.

The congressional district I represent changed dramatically for the 2012 election as a result of the 2010 census and the redistricting that followed. Fifty-five percent of the people in the newly created district had not been in the prior one. The geography changed dramatically as well, and my family decided to move from our home in Tacoma where we had lived for thirteen years. It was the only home our children had ever known.

The move and the effort to build my support in the new portions of my district required considerable effort for the better part of two years. We looked at houses for nine months, sold ours before we found a new one, and had to then find an apartment to fill the seven-week gap until we did buy and could move into our new house. I lost count of the boxes we packed and unpacked. My political team and I dove in and reached out to the new portions of the district, successfully building enough support to ward off serious opposition in the 2012 election and easily win a ninth term in the newly configured district.

This all counted as an unqualified success. I had no sense of foreboding as it all unfolded. I enjoyed it for the most part, working through whatever small frustrations popped up. It kept both my career and personal life on solid footing. I maintained my confidence that whatever steps I had or had not taken back in 2005 had worked. My life since then had clearly proved that point.

CHAPTER 7
The Anxiety Returns
FEBRUARY 2013

M y family returned home in late February of 2013 from a
vacation to Hawaii. Thirty-six hours after that, I flew back
to DC as Congress returned to session after the Presidents'
Day district workweek. I couldn't get to sleep that first
night back in DC. It wasn't because I felt anxious, but I simply
wasn't tired. Given the five-hour time difference between Hawaii
and DC, this inability to sleep should not have surprised me, but
there was something intangible beyond the obvious. Something
felt off. It worried me for reasons that I couldn't quite identify.

I shook it off and slept fine the next few nights. I returned to our new home in Bellevue on Thursday that same week. The next night, the same thing: I couldn't get to sleep. But again, the next few days I slept fine.

It hit me on the flight back to DC that following Monday morning—existential fear. I could feel my heart rate and pulse rapidly speed up. My mind raced, and my muscles tensed. My whole body suddenly perceived some profound threat to my very existence, like a doctor had just told me I had cancer. Or I looked up to see a mountain lion coming at me. Or my car was spinning out of control on an icy highway. Except, in the real world, as I sat in my seat on a calm and peaceful flight from SeaTac to Dulles, no such threat existed.

I tried to calm down, and for a few minutes here and there, I could. But the feeling of existential fear always came back. I would read a page or two in the book I was reading or just think about my plans for after we landed—catch a cab to the Capitol, vote, return a couple of calls, go over my calendar for the week. It didn't work. Imagine doing that while the mountain lion is coming at you. Yeah, okay, I guess I could worry about the mountain lion, but let's just stay positive. Maybe I'll catch a movie later or go to the gym. And I should really study that file my boss gave me. Not gonna happen when your whole body is focused on what it perceives to be a threat to your life.

I couldn't sleep that night in DC. The feeling of existential fear and all the symptoms remained firmly in place. The next morning, I visited the House physician's office. My blood pressure, normally checking in at around 110 over 70, hit 150 over

105. The doctor didn't offer much insight, seeming to assume that I would calm down eventually.

But why was I anxious in the first place? What was I anxious about? Every doctor loved to ask that question. I had no idea, even less than back in 2005. I did not feel the internalized fear of death I had felt back then. Now, my body had gone into full-scale fight-or-flight mode, and I could not even come close to identifying a specific threat.

Last time, back in 2005, I could feel the stress in my life building. I had fought the feeling that I couldn't handle it anymore, that raising two young children and being in Congress simply didn't work. This time, that was not the case. I was juggling a lot, but I enjoyed it. My conscious mind anyway would have said unequivocally that my life worked just fine.

One other difference showed up this time. The anxiety, in the days immediately following the initial attack, did let up a few times. The pressure would build relentlessly for a couple of days—no sleep, constant anxiety, an inability to eat. Then, a few times, it would release, like a balloon stretched to the maximum pressure point before finally, slowly letting out air and returning to a relaxed state. This relief never lasted longer than a few hours, however. The anxiety always returned with the same intensity.

I struggled through my life. I gave speeches, took meetings—did my job as best as I could. I proved to be relatively high functioning, able to speak coherently and follow conversations and discussions in meetings and hearings. Normally, I gave no outward sign of the extreme panic and anxiety coursing through my body, and I didn't tell anybody about it. I made excuses on the few occasions when I just couldn't calm down enough to handle a scheduled event. I canceled a lunch with Congressman Steny Hoyer, number two in House Democratic leadership, for this reason. He gave me a bad time about it later, just joking about how now that I was a big-shot committee ranking member I didn't have time for the likes of him. I smiled and went along with the joke.

I couldn't watch TV or read a book because I would stress about everything I saw or read. I know most people won't understand this, and I struggle to explain it even now, but when my anxiety kicked in, my mind seemed to go into overdrive on everything it saw or perceived. The more it saw or perceived, the harder it tried to work and the more intense the anxiety became. I would watch TV or read while in this state from time to time, but it always made things worse.

And my family. My God, my family. I shuddered every time I thought about trying to tell them what was going on with me. First of all, what the hell was going on with me? What could I say exactly? It's not like my wife didn't have enough stress going on in her life, trying to raise two children and running much of the household for all of us. I did tell her a little bit about it, but I always tried to minimize it—claiming it wasn't that bad and it would pass. How long could I get away with this explanation? I still helped out around the house—shuttling the children to various activities, helping with their homework. I barely slept. My heart and mind raced every night and the fear remained firmly in place, even as I pretended to be asleep so that my wife, lying next to me in bed, wouldn't worry about me—or at least not worry as much.

And I always had the same question. Now what?

CHAPTER 8
Back into the World of Drugs and Therapy

knew this was beyond my willpower, and I sought professional help after a few days. The psychologist I found at the University of Washington introduced me to cognitive behavioral therapy (CBT). I rejected the approach after just two sessions.

Five years and multiple therapists after this, I gained a much better understanding of CBT. But at first glance I dismissed it as telling me things I already knew. The theory, I believed, involved reducing your anxiety by understanding that the threats you were worried about, which can build like a snowball rolling downhill, weren't likely to actually happen. For instance, we stress about losing a job, losing a relationship, developing a horrible disease, or someone we love developing a horrible disease. But really, what were the odds of that actually happening?

My earlier headache example works in this regard. You can go from *Oh my God, I have a tumor!* to *My chances of having a tumor are less than one in a thousand, so therefore I'm fine.* I kind of already knew this, and for most of my life, I practiced it no problem, just not back in 2005 and not now. Now, every perceived threat seemed to overwhelm me regardless of the percentages, and focusing intently and logically on those percentages didn't change that. I also felt that the fear was the thing. The only thing I had to fear was fear itself, going back to FDR. So, okay, Doc, tell me, what are the percentage chances that when I go to bed tonight, I'm going to be gripped by a terrifying anxiety I cannot contain that has no explanation I can find? Based on the last week and a half at that point, really damn high.

The therapist and I also just didn't click. I learned, over the years, as I worked my way through my triple-digit number of healthcare providers, that this mattered and was not as easy to achieve as I, at first, had thought. They all come with their own personalities and hang-ups. I incorrectly assumed that being in a profession that required them to deal with all kinds of people would obligate them to adjust. Not so. It is important to try to find a doctor, chiropractor, physical therapist—whatever specialty—with whom you can connect based on your unique personality and theirs.

I, too rapidly, gave up on therapy and decided to pursue my pharmaceutical options. I wanted what I should have realized was not possible at this point—the quick fix. I rationalized this decision by believing it had worked back in 2005. I could just dabble in a little clonazepam for a month or two, fight through this odd anxiety outbreak, and soon get back to normal.

My doctor in DC, the House physician, agreed to this plan, and most times, when I took it, the clonazepam gave me relief. It never lasted more than a day, however, and I worried constantly about which days to take a pill and which days to not take a pill. Theoretically, at some point, just like in 2005 I would simply stop altogether. This thought stressed me out even more.

I explained this conflict to my doctor. He suggested I could stop worrying about the decision every day, and just take 0.5 milligrams every night. But what about side effects? Dependency? He assured me both were unlikely and that a whole lot of people in the world took benzodiazepines every day for years. I took this advice, and I tried hard to believe it. If I could just accept the fact that, for whatever reason, my body chemistry now required me to take this anti-anxiety medication every day, then I could get my life back. Over and over again, day after day, my mantra was *I just want my life back.*

Deep down, though, I never fully bought into this solution. I never really believed that this drug would solve my problem. This doubt did not, however, stop me from giving it a try. It worked okay for a few weeks until one night it didn't. I took the pill in the evening as usual and anxiety struck anyway, keeping me up most of the night. I was in DC, and I just lay on the couch in my office (my bed at that point, having tired of the Aerobed experience a couple of years earlier), hoping against hope that I would simply calm down and drift off to sleep. I didn't. My worries about dependency now exploded in my mind. I tried to stick to the plan, but without question, the 0.5 milligrams had become less dependable in its effectiveness. My doctor suggested yet another new plan. He gave me a different benzo, lorazepam, and suggested that a more stable course in treating my anxiety would be to transition me over to an SSRI—a selective serotonin uptake inhibitor. Prozac. Zoloft. That kind of thing.

I remembered the possibility of this drug from back in 2005. My doctor then suggested it as well, even wrote me a prescription for a few pills and handed me the bottle as we sat in his office. I held the container, rolling it around in my hand so the pills rattled. No, I decided then. This isn't me. I don't need this. I viewed taking pills as an unnecessary sign of weakness, a crutch I would then have to rely on for the rest of my life with highly unpredictable results.

This time, I followed the advice of my doctor. I took the lorazepam, and we settled on Zoloft for the SSRI. I took that for three days. And my anxiety spiked worse than it ever had. It was over the Memorial Day weekend. We had a couple over to our house for dinner, who had been good friends of ours for years, and I literally could not sit in the living room and talk. I felt so anxious I had to get up at one point and go for a walk in the neighborhood. I had never before been forced to be so obvious to other people about the impact of my anxiety. I usually kept outwardly functioning even as my heart raced and my insides churned. If I worried I wouldn't be able to, I canceled before people could see me, or if I started to feel completely overwhelmed at something with other people, I just made some plausible excuse for leaving early. But this time, I was sitting in my living room with my wife, our friends, and the five children we had between us. Where was I going exactly? I downplayed it as just a mild panic attack, but I could tell my wife and friends were concerned.

I stopped taking the Zoloft and the lorazepam, went back to the 0.5 milligrams of clonazepam, and somehow made it through the weekend. While others were at backyard barbecues or enjoying the mountains or beach, I worked placing calls to find someone who could help me. I managed to track down a doctor in Seattle who came highly recommended—an internist, not a psychiatrist, but he apparently had some experience in treating mental conditions as well as physical. I saw him on Wednesday, making the short walk up a steep hill after fighting my way through two meetings and a speech in downtown Seattle.

I was spent. Crushed by anxiety and exhaustion. I thought my life was over. I loved my life. All that work. All that I had accomplished. All the people who had sacrificed to help me in a thousand ways, including my wife and kids. How could I have wasted all of that? How would I ever get through this? I told the doctor small parts of my story in a fatalistic monotone, with little hope of a solution.

He assured me my life wasn't over. He had dealt with hundreds of people just like me. Busy people with complicated lives who reached a breaking point. He had no doubt I was fixable. This concept mattered to me and would continue to matter to me throughout my battle with anxiety and, later, physical pain.

I needed a path. I needed to believe I had a chance to get better. "Can you fix me?" How many times did I ask that question to how many different people during my struggle? I lost count.

"Okay." I let out a long breath. "What do we do?"

He recommended I see a psychiatrist, and he had one in mind. It was a guy who had an office just up the hill from where we sat. In the short term, he prescribed a slight boost in my clonazepam. I would keep taking the 0.5 at night and add 0.25 in the morning. Then I should transition off of that benzo and onto an SSRI. This I questioned, given my experience with Zoloft.

"You took too much too quickly," he said. "And Celexa is a much gentler SSRI. We will try that."

"Here's what I don't understand," I said. "Aren't things like Zoloft, Prozac—Celexa I've never heard of but I assume it's the same thing—don't they help with depression? Designed to ramp you up, not down?"

He explained that SSRIs balance out your serotonin. For anxiety, it takes three to six weeks to get that balance right. So, start with a low dose and build up. Start at 5 milligrams and get to a therapeutic dose, which should be around 20.

I trusted this plan—at least enough to give it a try. The boost in clonazepam helped immediately and gave me relative peace for the next few days as I built up the courage to dive into my SSRI experiment. The Celexa seemed okay as I worked my way up from 5 milligrams to 10. Then I hit 20.

My wife and I went to a wedding on a Saturday night in mid-June, back in our old hometown of Tacoma. We decided to do a late dinner at our favorite restaurant in the city after the wedding. I took my Celexa at the usual time that evening, right before we sat down to dinner. Thirty minutes later, an intense wave of anxiety poured over me, and I had an odd, deeply disturbing feeling in my brain that I can't fully explain. My heart started racing again, my stomach formed a permanent knot, and my mind fogged over in terror. The Celexa had clearly started messing with me in a very unhelpful way.

It continued to do this for the next two months. The clonazepam helped at times, and there were a few days mixed in when I thought maybe I was getting used to the SSRI, but overall it was an absolute nightmare of anxiety, insomnia, and the constant struggle to simply function from one moment to the next. My doctor explained this by saying that SSRIs can be "initially activating" for anxiety patients. That struck me as equivalent to saying that things could have gone better for Custer at the Little Big Horn. But I stuck with the drug, waiting for the magic moment when it would fully kick in and balance out my serotonin.

CHAPTER 9

My Second Psychiatrist and the Perils of Healthcare Policy

The new psychiatrist presented a different set of challenges—scheduling, payment, and a more serious effort at cognitive behavioral therapy. Scheduling, I know, sounds beside the point. You make the time in a crisis. You do what you have to do. It took me a while to recognize even this. I was overwhelmed already. That, in theory, was part of my problem. I didn't want to add to my troubles the problem of finding time every week for therapy. Again, I wanted a quicker fix. The hell of March, April, and May had pulled me past that point. I moved finding time for treatment much higher up on my priority list.

Still, there are only so many hours in the day, and I couldn't just stop doing my job or helping take care of my household. The psychiatrist also had a busy schedule and limited appointment times available. Finally, my traveling back and forth to DC added to the challenge of finding times that worked for both of us. I had to find a balance in my mind between the need to completely commit to the therapy while not becoming so obsessed with it that if two weeks went by where I couldn't get an appointment scheduled, I'd start freaking out about that.

The payment problems came from the fact that this psychiatrist didn't take insurance. This stretched our family budget and added to the scheduling issue in one sense. Okay, if I can't wedge in my weekly therapy, at least we save $200. Not a helpful thought when trying to commit to therapy.

I encountered this problem of healthcare providers not accepting insurance countless times as I sought help for my various conditions. The problem exists because of the incredible complexity all countries face in setting healthcare policy. It exists to the high degree it does in our country because the United States does a miserable job of addressing the problem. We could do a lot better, but I also want to caution against the notion that there is some magic solution. Here I will both borrow and paraphrase a line from a Malcolm Gladwell book I read called

Talking to Strangers. If I can convince you of only one thing on the subject of healthcare policy in our country, let it be this—healthcare policy is not easy.

Healthcare policy defies Adam Smith. Yes, I like using that line. My namesake's formulation on free markets envisioned two parties to transactions—a seller and a buyer. It also envisioned a level playing field between the two and a number of other things that often don't happen, but those problems are not my point here. Healthcare transactions, in most cases, have a seller, a buyer, and a separate payer—the healthcare insurance company. This third wheel at this particular party creates no end of problems.

Yes, insurance exists for other purposes, but usually those insurance purchases are made to guard against the occurrence of a very expensive, unlikely event. Flood insurance, windstorm insurance, earthquake insurance, life insurance (death is, of course, more than likely, but usually life insurance is a guard against an unexpected death). Car insurance doesn't even present the same problems as healthcare insurance because, again, you don't use that insurance too often. You don't use car insurance to pay for regular repairs, and most of us do our best to avoid more costly and unexpected accidents.

Health insurance gets used all the time, which sets up this constant battle—the seller would like to make money selling their product or service; the buyer wants that product or service to preserve or restore their good health; and the insurer, the one paying most if not all the cost of that product or service, would rather *not* pay. Please do pause and reflect on this last point.

Pretty much 100 percent of the time all insurers would rather not pay. Now, most of the time, they do pay because they are contractually and legally obligated to do so. But they will, with great frequency, search for ways to avoid this unhappy outcome. If your house gets flooded and you have flood insurance, you will likely fight a battle of some length to get the insurer to pay as much as you think they should. But almost nobody's house gets flooded very often. Healthcare does happen often. You get an annual physical. Women get breast-cancer screenings. Maybe you take medication for one thing or another. You get sick. You hurt yourself while engaged in some form of physical activity. It happens all the time.

And, again, 100 percent of the time, your health insurer would rather not pay. I'm lucky. My wife is both brilliant and tenacious. She loves accounting issues and hates with an absolute passion paying one penny more than she should have to pay for anything. She battles health insurers with some frequency, and though she is not always successful, if I were to bet on her and give the points in all these battles, I'd wind up money ahead.

The seller in these transactions, healthcare providers, fight these battles as well, trying to get a given health insurance company to pay for a product or service the seller has provided or wants to provide to the buyer. There are many different insurance companies, public and private, and what they cover and don't varies a lot from one to the other. They don't even let every provider into their network. This means that if you change insurance companies for one reason or another, your doctor may no longer be covered by your insurance.

My psychiatrist did not want to fight these battles. He ran a lean shop. He was a solo practitioner and shared a four-suite office space with three other solo-practicing psychiatrists where they also shared a scheduler/admin. Not taking insurance helped him keep his overhead low.

This insurance challenge for many providers, however, stems from a much more fundamental problem than the accounting challenges of meeting the demands of varying health insurers. Society recognizes both that healthcare is a necessity and that only a very few people can ever hope to be able to pay for the cost of all the healthcare they will need, much less want. We have to have a healthcare insurance system. But the demand for healthcare products and services far outstrips the amount of money available to pay for it. Choices must be made regardless of the healthcare system, meaning that each system must answer two fundamental questions: What will insurance pay for, and who will make that decision?

If you think this sounds easy, consider just two realities of this difficult choice. First, advancements in medicine have driven the cost of healthcare up significantly. Kidney dialysis is the easiest example. Prior to the development of this technology, if you developed kidney disease you were not a problem for our healthcare system. You died, which was sad but not that expensive. Now you get kidney dialysis and stay alive. The latest google search I did says that roughly 500,000 people in America get this treatment three times a week. The cost estimate for each patient is $100,000 a year. There are hundreds of other examples of new treatments that have been discovered in the last seventy years or so that have driven up the cost of healthcare dramatically. The system has to somehow absorb that.

Second, not all treatments are as widely accepted as dialysis. Let's say someone with a PhD in psychology independently develops a new treatment for anxiety and decides the treatment requires a patient to be seen for an hour five days a week at $175 an hour. Should insurance pay for that? What about acupuncture? Chiropractors? Naturopaths? I eventually wound up seeing muscle-treatment people who had developed a variety of methods: rolfing, the Bowen method, myofascial release, dry needling (every little bit as painful as it sounds, by the way), and muscle-activation therapy. Should insurance pay for all of this? And remember that insurance only works if some people are paying *more* in premiums than they take out in services. The math very quickly fails to add up.

Many people I work with, at this point in the conversation, say things like "That's why we need a single-payer healthcare system." Or "That's why I support Medicare for all." Or "We should have Canada's healthcare system." I support universal access to healthcare. I am a cosponsor of Medicare for all. Personally, I lean more toward the healthcare systems in countries like France and Germany—everybody is covered, strong government mandate and regulations, not single payer. But any of these systems would be an improvement over the chaos of our current system, where we pay more per capita for healthcare than any other nation in the world by a comfortable margin but consistently rank in the mid thirties on the quality of the care provided.

Just don't go thinking these other systems would somehow get us to the point where nobody would be denied healthcare they either need or think they need. Brutal choices remain, regardless of the system. No society can pay for everything. Somebody must decide what gets covered and what doesn't.

Better, I believe, to have a system where experts analyze data and make informed decisions instead of the Wild, Wild West approach we use in the United States right now, but nothing would be flawless or allow everybody to get everything.

Please look up the thoughts and writings of surgeon and public-health researcher Dr. Atul Gawande, and read *The Healing of America*, by T. R. Reid, for much more in-depth and informed details on healthcare policy, but for now, believe me.

Healthcare policy is not easy.

CHAPTER 10
If at First You Don't Succeed . . .

paid my psychiatrist out of pocket and did my best to find time in my schedule to see him once a week while also taking both clonazepam and Celexa. My psychiatrist, for his part, tried cognitive behavioral therapy on me. CBT involved more than just learning helpful percentages. I needed to carefully identify exactly what made me anxious, to name it, as the lingo went. I made a list and then, as homework, I had to track my anxiety and attempt to tie it to something specific. Then we discussed those something specifics.

The specifics were the pressure of being responsible for my children. How do we make sure they do well in school? How could I help them choose the right activities and get along with their friends? My concerns about juggling those responsibilities with the responsibilities of my job, and worries about my health, were among those we discussed, anxiety being the big one but also my physical ailments—bad back, sore knee, pain in my right foot, my problematic digestive system. I discussed the overwhelming pressure I felt to meet my responsibilities, the sense of frustration and stress that would come over me when I couldn't, like when Congress had an unexpected change in its voting schedule, and I had to choose between missing votes and canceling planned activities with my family.

None of this helped me very much. The better question would have been not what makes me anxious but why those things made me *so* anxious. Why would something in my brain cause these basic life pressures to trigger that primal fight-or-flight instinct connected to a perceived existential threat? My psychiatrist did mention this issue in one sense. He identified this overreaction on my part as something the mental-health field calls "catastrophizing." He incorrectly decided, however, that he could get me to stop doing it just by showing me the illogic of it and telling me to stop. But my reaction seemed beyond my control, beyond the basic rules of logic as I understood them at the time, and he didn't attempt to go deeper to get at this more fundamental problem.

I also, once again, did not bond with my therapist. His lean approach to his overhead gave the distinct impression he viewed his work much more like a profit-making business than an enterprise designed to help people. I got that it had to be both, but the balance seemed off. I also worried that we weren't "clicking," which means that I worried that he didn't like me that much. I cared a great deal at that point in my life what other people thought of me. Still do, though in a much healthier manner. It's a useful trait in a politician when it doesn't get out of hand. I often went off, during my sessions, telling stories to my psychiatrist that I thought illustrated the way my anxiety happened and impacted me. He seemed impatient with these stories, like I was getting him off track from his plan.

This made me wonder if he didn't like me because of my politics. I worried about this from time to time as I sought help from various healthcare providers. They all knew who I was, usually right when they met me but, obviously, always once I explained what I did for a living. I hoped, being in Seattle, I'd be on safe ground as a Democrat. I am, however, a center-left Democrat. So, maybe not far enough left? Plus, a lot of doctors are Republicans. They tend to make a lot of money, so they don't like taxes, and they don't like being sued or paying high insurance premiums for liability. I thought I was reasonable on both these issues, but still, I was a Democrat. Dumb things to be thinking about when seeking therapy, I realize, but it was what it was.

I also found with this psychiatrist and about half of the other therapists I saw over the years an odd tendency to greet information about my challenges with a look that seemed to me to be saying, *Wow, you are insane!*

I explained to this psychiatrist early on how much clonazepam I had taken since the onset of my symptoms over three months prior. I told him the exact amount, for how many days I had taken that amount, and also listed the days in those time periods when I switched up and took a little more or a little less. He shook his head. "I have never had a patient who has been able to give me such an exact accounting of the medication they have taken day-by-day." He also had little patience with my constant worrying about this drug. He found it unhelpful that I was constantly changing up how much I thought I should take as I swung wildly from my fear of becoming addicted to it to my fear of the anxiety being too great if I wasn't taking it. He seemed to find these actions wrong of me.

Okay, I thought. *Isn't this kind of the point? If I wasn't a little bit off, I wouldn't be paying $200 a pop for these fifty-minute sessions.* Fifty minutes, by the way, not an hour. He was always very clear on that.

More than once after responses from him like the above, I had the distinct impression that what he was really thinking was *You are bonkers. Sucks to be you. But hey, we have to wrap this up. I've got a tee time in an hour.*

This description isn't really fair, I know. It merely shows my level of frustration and desperation at this point. June and July that year were brutal months for me as the Celexa worked on my brain. I barely slept, and that fog of terror permeated my being, day in and day out. I woke every morning more and more convinced there was no way out. I had failed. I would never get my life back.

My visits to my psychiatrist became more infrequent as we moved into August, and I worked with my other doctor, the internist, to get off of the clonazepam. I did that way too quickly and apparently before the Celexa "kicked in" to start helping me.

I did a CODEL to Afghanistan at the end of August right after I stopped taking clonazepam altogether. Not a wise choice. The anxiety I felt on that trip was brutal and had nothing to do with any fear of getting shot or blown up by the Taliban. I kept this reality hidden from all on the trip except for my Armed Services Committee staff director. I managed to survive, though I did panic-text my internist more than once, expressing the firm belief that I would not. I literally texted him at one point, "I feel like I'm going to die." He wrote back, quite sensibly, "You are not going to die." And I didn't.

Then, on September 12, 2013, the anxiety disappeared, twenty-eight days after I took my last benzo. Apparently, for all the hell of getting used to the Celexa, 20 milligrams of it was what I needed. However, three weeks later, my anxiety returned in full force. Ten days after that it disappeared again. I struggled to identify anything in my life that impacted when the anxiety came and when it went. My stressful life continued—going back and forth to DC, dealing with political conflict like that fall's government shutdown—family illness and arguments—but none of it seemed to track with my up-and-down anxiety.

The answer may not have been clear at that point no matter how I looked at it, but clues did appear, clues I failed to recognize in great enough detail at the time.

I took a trip to the Democratic Republic of the Congo the first week of December that year. My trip there in 2009 had connected me to an NGO that worked in the country. They sponsored my 2013 trip. Anxiety gripped me in the days leading up to my departure from DC. I boarded the late-morning flight out of Dulles, and that anxiety melted away. I slept one of my more peaceful eight hours in some time on that flight to Addis Ababa. The calm remained as I navigated my way through the airport and found my connecting flight to Kinshasa. It was the first time I had ever been in that airport. I was alone, the rest of the people on the trip having already arrived in the DRC. But I was perfectly at peace.

We did a few meetings in the city after I arrived and then had dinner with a team of US State Department people stationed in Kinshasa. The dinner was light, for some reason, and by the time I tried to get to sleep back in my hotel room, I was still hungry, without any options for getting something to eat. My anxiety returned and so did my insomnia. The next day was a full itinerary: flying up to and touring a dam project on the Congo River with a large group of people, and then attending other meetings back in the capital. It was a living hell. I was so tired I kept nodding off every time we sat in a bus or a plane, and the fog of terror was as intense as it had ever been.

I finally begged off the last two meetings of the day and returned to the hotel. I knew one person on the trip fairly well. She had formed the NGO and was from Seattle. I confided in her my problem, and she helped me get some drugs. I viewed it as my only option. I tried the Ambien first. I slept for four solid hours but woke up a little before midnight and felt the anxiety still hanging in me. I turned to my old reliable friend—benzodiazepines. Klonopin, another name for clonazepam, brought me peace once again. The rest of the trip went fine. I sat in the lounge in the Frankfurt airport for five hours during our layover on the trip home and caught up on five days' worth of emails without a hint of anxiety.

Why did something as simple as being a bit hungry on an overseas trip trigger such a severe outbreak of anxiety? It isn't unusual. You do a multiple time-zone change, and your body clock gets messed up. You don't sleep well and get hungry at odd times. Been there, done that—many times, both before and since this one trip. I viewed it as a threat, I now believe, because anything that made it less likely that I would be able to perform as expected—to meet my responsibilities and accomplish my goals—worried me greatly.

Oh my God. I think my back is going out. I have to take Jack to soccer and pick up Kendall from dance. And I'm flying back to DC tomorrow morning. Multiple hearings and meetings all week. What if I can't do it? Oh my God. I'm hungry. I won't be able to get to sleep. I'll be too tired to do my meetings tomorrow. I can't fail. What can I do? A lot of things can be a trigger in this mindset. Anything that made success less likely created in my mind an outsized sense of the possibility of failure. And failure was unacceptable.

I nearly failed in carrying out a major legislative challenge back in 1994 while in the state Senate. My caucus charged me, as the chair of the Law and Justice Committee, with passing our top legislative priority in that year's short, sixty-day session— juvenile justice reform. It became a massive bill and contained hot-button issues like gun control and sentencing reform. We got to conference and then stalled as I battled with my House counterpart to try to get a deal. That deal finally came mere hours before the sixty-day deadline. Then the conference re-port failed by 11 votes when we brought it up in the Senate.

Democrats had a 28–21 majority, but we lost 10 of them on the vote. We walked off the floor and into one of those come-to-Jesus caucus meetings where we all yell at each other about whose fault the failure had been. But I knew. It was mine. It was my job to deliver this bill, and I had failed.

I tried to explain to the caucus, when the majority leader gave me the chance to speak, how we had gotten to this point, but midway through I broke down and started crying uncontrollably. Several of my colleagues had to comfort me to get me to calm down. We regrouped, immediately called a special session, and passed the bill two days later, and whatever may have happened in caucus, the incident did not trigger any kind of anxiety attack. But it clearly showed just how my perception of any kind of failure impacted me.

CHAPTER 11

Drugs–Can't Live with Them, Struggling to Live Without Them

returned home from my trip to the DRC that December in 2013 and continued taking my 20 milligrams of Celexa every day. I also made the questionable decision to, during periods when the Celexa didn't seem to be working and I just couldn't take the anxiety anymore, take a clonazepam pill to buy me twenty-four hours of peace. I had a decent supply of the 0.5 milligram pills from back when I had been taking it consistently. I still worried obsessively about taking these medications. I wanted guarantees. I wanted to know for sure that taking a given medication in a given dose would cure my anxiety while at the same time not creating dependency or adverse side effects. The world doesn't work that way, of course, but that reality didn't stop me from worrying about it and wishing that the world did work that way.

I sought reassurance wherever I might find it. My doctors, as I've mentioned, did their best to answer my questions and give me that reassurance. I also started thinking about the people around me. I would sit in a meeting and look at the ten or fifteen people there and wonder how many of them took some kind of anti-anxiety or antidepressant medication. Statistically, I knew the number had to be reasonably high. They seemed fine. But how could I really know that? I knew they could be looking back at me and thinking, *Hmm, he seems fine.*

I also stumbled into troubling information. I met with a nonprofit in my district that worked with troubled youth. They ran a bunch of programs, but at one point they brought up the problem of too many troubled young people being put on anti-depressant drugs like Prozac. They questioned the rash decision of doctors to go too quickly to a solution with troubling side effects. I kept my thoughts on the subject to myself as I listened nervously.

I did come across people close to me who had experience with taking medication for anxiety or depression, or who knew somebody who did. Those discussions didn't help either. It worked for some, didn't work for others, and was a mixed bag for most.

Then I made the mistake of seeking reassurance online. Don't get me wrong, it wasn't hard to find reassurance online. Dozens of people posted rave reviews about Celexa: *It changed my life. Best decision I ever made. No side effects. Quick relief of my anxiety/depression.* I also found people who swore any concerns about clonazepam were overblown. *I've taken 2 milligrams a day for twenty years. Cured my anxiety and no side effects.*

First, however, I wondered about all of these positive reviews. I knew enough about the pharmaceutical industry to be suspicious. I could easily picture an army of interns at the company that makes Celexa hunched over their keyboards, cranking out these rave reviews.

Second, not all of the reviews were positive. It was just like trying to pick a plumber by checking Yelp reviews. You read two glowing recommendations and think *Great, I'll go with Bob's plumbing.* But hey, look. *There's a third review. Let's just click on that to be sure. Yikes. This guy says Bob's overcharges, does shoddy work, showed up four hours late, and the customer found jewelry missing after Bob's people left.*

The Internet had no end of SSRI/benzo horror stories. One site existed dedicated to spreading the message that benzos were little better than swallowing poison. Addiction comes quickly, side effects are brutal, and (this stat resonated with me in a bad way) if you come off the drug too fast, you can mess up your mind for life. I asked my psychiatrist about this, the possibility that clonazepam caused brain damage. He shook his head and said no with a look like he found the idea absurd. But what if he was wrong? I threw the last of my clonazepam away and decided to just stick with the 20 milligrams of Celexa.

I also stressed about my approach to, and the importance of, meditation. My brain was broken, right? I had to do some things differently in my life to fix it. Drugs freaked me out, but meditation was just about the most drug-free, natural thing in the world. Maybe, if I just got that right, it would be all good. But what did it mean to get meditation right? Most every book I had ever read on meditation, and everybody I asked about it, emphasized that it was just something you did, not something you had to do in some certain specific way. That was the whole point. Relax. Let your mind just exist. I don't have to do any-thing, right? Like my first psychiatrist back in 2005 kept trying to convince me.

I had tried several methods of meditation, moving past the initial approach of simply reciting the Peace Prayer of Saint Francis, but for the most part I came back to the basic effort of sitting in a chair and simply breathing, in and out, while counting the breaths—up to ten and then starting over at one. I learned the idea wasn't to eliminate all thought—apparently one has to do this a lot and be really relaxed to get to that point—but to let those thoughts come and go. Just notice the thought; don't pursue it or analyze it. There are no good or bad thoughts. They just come and go. The same for sounds or other sensations in the world around you as you meditate. You don't have to get to the point where you don't hear those sounds; just don't let them distract you.

To what end? I guessed at the time this was an effort to both rest your mind and to focus it—to help in the all-important meditative goal of *being present*. I had never been very good at being present. I was a planner, remember? Always thinking about what came next. Some of my best insights about dealing with personal challenges and achieving professional goals came to me while I was doing something else. I was always thinking. I had perceived this as a strength.

But now? Okay, I'm eating this burrito. That's what I'm doing. So, I guessed being present meant I had to focus on eating, and hopefully enjoying, the burrito. But why couldn't I be eating the burrito and working through in my mind what I should say in my speech coming up after lunch to the local Chamber of Commerce?

It's a balance I now understand. As with all things life, one needs to both think and focus. Meditation helps train your mind to be able to do this. To not be distracted. I can eat my burrito and think about my speech, but don't let some thought about a question that I might not have a great answer to distract me so much that I both don't enjoy the burrito and don't give a good speech.

I kept worrying at the time, however, about not being able to focus perfectly. I would go a moment or two in my meditation and really feel my thoughts simply and easily focused on my breathing and nothing else. *I'm doing it,* my mind would think. *Hooray for me.* Then I'd be distracted by this self-congratulatory thought. Damn. Back to square one.

I also heard from a number of people that the ultimate goal of meditation was to get to the point where you could separate your spirit from your body. Out-of-body experiences or "flying," as I have sometimes heard it called. People who achieve such a perfect meditative state that they literally feel as if they are floating around the room and looking back at their body sitting in the chair.

I remembered a young woman I met back in 1983, my freshman year in college at Western Washington University in Bellingham. She was a freshman as well, and we lived in the same dorm. She quickly developed a reputation for being a bit odd. She put these triangles up all around her room, reportedly designed to ward off evil spirits, and spent an entire day one time in a state of panic because some evil beast had broken in. I think because somebody took down a triangle.

I walked into the common room one evening and found her lying on one of the couches. We exchanged hellos, and I asked how her day had been. "Exhausting," she responded. "I had to go to LA to help a friend who was in trouble." I nodded sympathetically and then remembered I had seen her fairly late that morning in the dining hall. How could she have so quickly flown to LA and back? She saw the confused look on my face and spoke before I could ask. "I did it spiritually. I left my body here. It is always just so exhausting when I have to do that for any length of time."

I had thought about this exchange often since it happened, and I honestly didn't think she was making it up. It is possible, of course, that she suffered from some bipolar disorder and had lost touch with reality. But who knows? She never struck me that way in general, not that I was any kind of an expert on the subject.

This memory and the other things I had heard about how far meditation could take you both gave me hope—hey, maybe there is a spiritual realm where one can find peace separate from the burdens of physical existence—and made me think I had a lot more work to do on the meditation front. I dove deeper into the possible options and discovered a thing called Transcendental Meditation, or TM. People all over the world, including in Bellevue, Washington, offered courses to train others how to do it.

I paid $950 for something like four weeks of TM sessions, I forget exactly how many. A small group of us, seven or eight, met in a house and learned how to meditate. This type of meditation involved sitting for twenty minutes twice a day and concentrating on a specific mantra, unique to each individual, with your eyes closed. You let thoughts come and go but always came back to the mantra. The last session, we each went off separately to a room with a teacher who led us through a formal ceremony involving a few physical items I can't now remember and some chants. Finally, I was given my mantra.

I worried, throughout these sessions, about the Celexa I was taking. Might that interfere with my path to spiritual enlightenment? I asked my teacher this on my last day as we sat down, and he prepared to perform the ritual of giving me my mantra. No, he assured me. That was no problem at all. He himself, in fact, was taking an SSRI. Had been for over ten years.

I kept my thoughts on this revelation to myself and completed my training. But that had pretty much done it for me. I was doing all this so that I could train my mind to stop torturing me without me having to take some drug I didn't trust. *You have got to be kidding me!* was what I really wanted to say to the guy when he told about taking an SSRI. If my teacher, or yogi I guess is the correct term, can't achieve a level of spiritual enlightenment without popping a bunch of modern-day pharmaceuticals, then what the hell chance did I have?

So, it was just me, my Celexa, and my psychiatrist's efforts at CBT. I had to hope that these three things could somehow combine to bring me peace. But it wasn't working.

I'm a huge sports fan. I won't attempt to justify that. I will state as fact that the success or failure of the sports teams I root for has always had an impact on my happiness. I've mellowed on this a bit with age, still finding joy in the outcome of sporting events but trying not to despair when things go poorly. I am a Seattle Mariners fan after all, and that kind of requires either this outlook or a strong masochistic streak.

This is how bad things had gotten for me in early 2014. The Seattle Seahawks, another of my favorite teams, won the Super Bowl that year. The Celexa, or whatever, worked well enough for me to somewhat enjoy the Seahawks beating San Francisco to make it to the Super Bowl. It will always bring joy to my heart to rewatch Richard Sherman batting that ball into Malcolm Smith's hands for the game-sealing interception. But I was gone with anxiety two weeks later when they crushed the Broncos to win the Super Bowl. It brought me no joy at all. I watched, swallowed up by that fog of terror that I knew only too well. I couldn't get through it to even really focus on the game.

I kept riding this roller coaster for another month and then decided, *Enough! Clearly, this isn't working.* My doctor and my psychiatrist suggested that maybe I needed a higher dose of Celexa. I tried to creep up to 30 milligrams, but that only made things worse. They then offered the suggestion that many people battle to find the right dose of the right SSRI. We could try a different SSRI. Uh, yeah. Let me think about that for a second. Hell, no. Start over? Go back to June and July when the "initial activation" of Celexa brought me to my knees? That's a hard pass.

I suggested a different plan. I would get off the Celexa altogether and bury the idea that SSRIs could help me. Then I would go back on 0.75 milligrams of clonazepam and do a slow, steady taper off of it. I took seriously the idea that me coming off too fast the first time might have caused some lasting damage to my brain. Maybe, if I did it right, I could correct that. I read that the best approach was to drop 10 percent on your dose every fourteen days. I would try that. It would take four months, but I would continue my therapy and maybe get to the drug-free peace that I wanted so badly. My doctors agreed to this plan.

Plans rarely, however, stay exactly the same as when you first develop them. You tinker. You try to find ways to make small improvements. I tinkered with my titration schedule to get off of the clonazepam while also worrying about how to get more out of my therapy. There is, however, a fine line here between smart, tactical changes to a plan and way, crazy overthinking things to the point of paralysis and dysfunction. The challenge in finding this balance always reminds me of a joke I heard a comedian tell one time. He was talking about the difficulty of getting the attention of someone you are attracted to in a bar, and how he had been told that eye contact was the key. But he discovered that "There's a fine line between eye contact and the piercing stare of a psychopath."

My approach to the clonazepam titration more closely resembled the piercing stare of a psychopath. It made me nervous.

I wanted to be drug free, the sooner the better. So, why fourteen days? What if I did twelve? I'd be done quicker. And the 10 percent drop wasn't really possible because of the limited dosage amounts commercially available, so I had to think through how far I would drop from one step to the next.

The pills only came in certain amounts, 0.5 milligrams being the main one. You could also get the drug in a 0.25 and a 0.125, but those amounts did not come in a pill you swallowed. You put the tablet under your tongue and let it dissolve. This meant that from 0.75, you could only really go down to 0.625. I could also go the specialty pharmacy route where they custom-make pills to whatever dose desired, but that was expensive, not covered by insurance, and I wondered if the different way the pill was made might somehow change how my body processed the drug. Finally, I could go the drug dealer route—get a razor blade and try to carve up a 0.5 pill into some specific amount.

There was so much here for me to obsess about, it's hard to know where to start in explaining the weird, freak-out decisions I made as I bounced all over the place on the exact right approach. So I won't.

Suffice to say that my psychiatrist, to his credit, told me to knock it off. Set a schedule and stick to it. Fourteen days in between steps. And don't obsess about the 10 percent thing. Go down as the pill sizes allow. If we get to the point where you have to carve up a pill, we will deal with it then, but that's a couple months away.

Overall, my drug plan was working okay. I loved the initial twenty-eight days back on 0.75 milligrams of clonazepam, and I sure didn't miss the Celexa. I hit bumps in the road once

I started over-worrying the steps down, but I was still in a lot better shape than I had been. I might have a bad day or two during a step-down, instead of the week or two of hell that kept smacking me when I was taking Celexa.

CHAPTER 12
Trying to Correct the Past

did feel a strong need to pursue a different therapy strategy because CBT did not seem to be getting me where I needed to go. I kept learning more and more about psychotherapy and repressed emotions/experiences. Many believed that traumatic experiences from as far back as childhood could cause emotional problems in adults. These experiences were just too painful, so your mind refused to think about them, and in many cases, children don't yet have the cognitive ability to process traumatic events.

You kept those memories clamped down in your subconscious. But like steam trying to escape from a kettle, if it had no easy way to get out, it would find another, more damaging and explosive escape route. This could manifest in adults in a variety of mental health problems, including depression and anxiety.

Treatment focused on bringing those painful memories out into the open, to have the patient talk about them and to the greatest extent possible experience those repressed emotions. To allow the steam out in a more recognizable and manageable manner. *Maybe,* I thought, *this was what that first psychiatrist I had seen back in 2005 was trying to get at.*

I met a woman around this time, an army veteran with a PhD in psychology. She was working on ways to help veterans with PTSD in this way. But she had also been through therapy herself, having dealt with an alcoholic father and being sexually assaulted while in the military. She described a process where the therapist guided the patient to mentally go back to the moment of this trauma—in some cases, even using hypnosis to make the memory as real and in the moment as possible. She described the incredible emotional pain of reliving some of the most devastating experiences of your life, but she also said that, once addressed, a person's ability to deal with the world now around them increased dramatically. She connected this therapy with a strong emphasis on using meditation to help teach your mind how to deal with stressful situations, to train it to not go chasing after every troubling thought. I found this fascinating and, since I worked a lot with the military, wanted to find ways to fold this type of treatment into helping our veterans with PTSD.

But as for it helping me in any way, I had two problems with seeing it as a possible solution. First, I didn't have any trauma that I could think of, as a child or at any other time. I didn't have an alcoholic parent. I hadn't ever been sexually or physically abused. I viewed trauma as something big and significant. I had met with so many people over the years who had suffered what I viewed as real trauma—the experiences listed above and far, far worse. People abused as children, abandoned, passed from one foster home to another, or forced to live with drug-addicted caregivers. I honestly thought it beyond presumptuous for me to blame my current problems on some "trauma" I had experienced when so many people had truly suffered.

Second, on the things that did trouble me from my childhood, I wasn't suppressing them. I talked about my father's death. The guilt I felt over my relationship with my mother and about her death. My conflicts with my brother. The discovery of my adoption. I was very open about this stuff with my wife and friends, always had been. Repression didn't seem to be an issue.

I don't remember exactly what convinced me to give it a try. The woman recommended a therapist who worked out of McLean, Virginia. The therapist, a female psychologist, specialized in this type of psychotherapy. I stopped seeing my psychiatrist in Seattle and made an appointment to see the psychologist in Virginia.

My new therapist let out a short sigh. "You do realize you are beating yourself up for beating yourself up, don't you?"

I closed my eyes and leaned back slightly in my chair, realizing both the truth of what she said and the stupidity of me doing it. We had been discussing my obsession with doing everything right, never making a mistake, and, when I did, how badly I felt the need to try to find some way to fix it. This line of thinking extended to me wanting to get my therapy right, and one of her instructions had been to stop being so hard on myself. Yet here I sat, telling her about mistakes I had made in the week since I last saw her. A workout I did that wound up hurting my back. Staying up later than I should have and then struggling to quell my anxiety and get to sleep. A series of minor, inconsequential things that I somehow blew up into major impediments to me getting better. Then, of course, I took the final step, apologizing and criticizing myself for beating myself up over these mistakes.

"Do you expect to be perfect?" she asked.

"Of course not. I mean, come on, nobody's perfect, right?" I paused, unsure where to take this thought, then decided to just wait for the next question. My therapist stared back at me with a pleasant, patient look on her face.

Reporters and therapists, I thought, *both hoping I would feel compelled to fill the silence if they just outwaited me.* I knew this trick only too well. But here, of course, the very kind, soft-spoken, middle-aged woman sitting across from me in the office she had set up in the basement of her house in the upper-middle-class suburb of McLean wasn't trying to lure me into saying something I shouldn't. She was trying to help me.

"I expect to succeed at a high level," I said finally. "I guess that's how I would put it. Not be perfect exactly."

"Why?"

"I guess I see the problem you're getting at. It's like I'm trying to get back up to a 4.0 after getting a B. Can't be done. I can't correct every mistake."

"That's true. And it puts pressure on you that you can never really release." I nodded, acknowledging her point. "But why do you feel that pressure in the first place?"

"I don't know. I just do. You might as well be asking why I feel the necessity to breathe." She held my gaze and didn't say anything, a look of infinite patience on her face. I liked this therapist. She seemed calm, kind, and quite confident in what she was doing at all times. I hadn't seen much of that in my previous experiences with therapists.

"My father, I guess," I said finally, then paused again. The patient look remained on her face as if permanently etched. I wondered briefly if she had to practice it in the mirror or if she more or less had it down by this point. "He pushed me," I added. "Always seemed to want me to do something big with my life but didn't quite seem to know how to do it. Neither did I, for that matter."

"Can you give me an example?"

I considered the question for a moment and then said, "College. Where I went. Where he wanted me to go. It's complicated."

"I'm sure it is."

"Okay. I kind of slacked off in high school. Grades weren't as good as they should have been. I could tell it bugged my father, but he never really said much about it. Neither of my parents had college degrees. And my older brother. Well, no way he was going to college, but it had always somehow been expected of me. I was fine with that, but I had a 3.2 GPA, and not that much money. So I found the options limited. And I was really nervous about it, like I was with everything." We had discussed at length my fears and lack of confidence growing up.

"But I was editor-in-chief of my high school newspaper and I thought I wanted to be a journalist at that point in my life. This helped me focus on a couple of options. First, Western Washington. Nice. Safe. Cheap. Good reputation as a journalism school. And, bizarrely, Northwestern. How the hell am I getting into a school like Northwestern? Well, they had a really good journalism school as well, and I won a few awards on that high school newspaper. And that's where my father wanted me to go. But I got waitlisted.

"I guess I could have pushed harder to get into Northwestern after that, gone there and done an interview like they asked me to, but it didn't really make sense to me. Crazy expensive and I was terrified of doing the two-hour drive up to Bellingham so how the hell was I going to make it in Chicago?" I paused to take a breath. "Western's in Bellingham," I explained. "And yeah, Evanston, not Chicago," I added, correcting myself on Northwestern's location. "Anyway, I took my name off the waitlist at Northwestern and went to Western.

"I wound up having a good time there. I had been delivering newspapers since I was eleven, so I had enough in savings that I didn't have to work, given how cheap housing and tuition were. I drank more than I should have, got pretty good grades, and more or less enjoyed the experience."

"How did your father feel about it?"

I frowned but didn't immediately respond. She continued looking at me. "That's the weird thing. We really didn't communicate that much. But I sensed he felt I should do more. I felt it, too. So, I transferred to Fordham after my freshman year. I had to challenge myself. New York City, right? If you can make it there you can make it anywhere?"

"Why Fordham?"

"Friend I had in high school. Originally from New York. Family moved to SeaTac when the friend and I were both sophomores in high school. We met, became friends. Then his family moved back to New York, and my friend went to Fordham. Opened my mind up to the possibility." I smiled at the memory. "That my father liked. Me going to Fordham. Even though, again, how in the hell was I going to pay for it? Not as expensive as Northwestern, but way more expensive than Western."

I started to explain the finances in more detail, but then I smiled again. "That Thanksgiving, the first year I was at Fordham, I came home and my father and I stayed up until two in the morning just talking. He grew up in Rhode Island. Spent time in New York City. It was like we finally had something to talk about." I paused as the smile left my face and I looked down. "Four months later, he died."

"How did that make you feel?"

I looked back at her like *You're kidding, right?* "Not good," I said eventually. "Yes," I added, "obviously it made me feel like I would never have the chance to prove to my father that he had been right to push. Right to think I could make something of myself." We sat in silence for almost a minute before I said, "I had this dream one night. Six months or so after I got elected to the state Senate. Incredibly vivid dream. My father and I were getting the newspaper from just outside our front door. The news about my election was plastered all over the front page. And yes, he was very proud of me. That I guess is the biggest failure that I feel."

She frowned, a confused look on her face. "Not that," I said. "Not that my father died before I could prove myself. The failure of my whole family. They never really seemed happy. My brother went off the deep end when I was about twelve. My parents' health failed. It was just one big mess."

"Is that your failure or your family's?" she asked.

I thought about this for a few seconds, unsure at first of what I really believed, then said simply, "Both. I mean, why didn't they tell me I was adopted?" I added, focusing on the family's side of the blame. "According to my biological mother, they were supposed to. That had to be a ton of pressure on them. Surely, people around us knew. What if I accidentally found out? And why didn't I find out? How clueless could I have been?

"My wife's family? Five children. They talk all the time about the circumstances of each child's birth. How my mother-in-law experienced her pregnancies. My family? Never talked about it. And I knew I was born in Washington, DC. This didn't clue me in? Who goes on vacation to the other side of the country to give birth?"

I went on explaining why I viewed my family life growing up as a failure. My mother was never happy that I could recall. My brother was a disaster. My father seemed anxious and frustrated much of the time. I learned, after he died, that he had joined the Navy at the age of seventeen in 1943. He tested high enough on his entrance exam to qualify for Officer Candidate School and get sent to Princeton for training. He dropped out after one semester for reasons I never found out, but I knew how smart he was. He read constantly, and I grew up thinking that everybody's father had the answer to every question because mine did. What was he doing living in a trailer and taking bags on and off of airplanes? Questions I would never be able to ask."

"Why do you see yourself as responsible for the failure of your family?"

"I was supposed to be the smart one, right? Okay grades. Decent athlete. We all knew my older brother had issues. But why couldn't I do something to make our family happier? To make us get along better?"

I thought about all of this in silence for a minute or two. I felt trapped in a circular argument of anger and guilt. I had never really buried the frustration and shame I felt during my years growing up. The memories pained me still. And then anxiety overwhelmed me in the here and now. Was that anxiety somehow caused by those painful childhood experiences and my memories of them? Why did my parents let this happen? Why did my birth parents both abandon me and drop me into what turned out to be a dysfunctional situation?

Then I felt guilty. It's easy to blame other people, but okay, smart guy, what did you do to make your family better? I did not do nearly enough to help my mother after my father died, that I knew. How could I blame them and not hold myself accountable? And my life worked out fine. Great even. My parents weren't so lucky. How was that fair? Then I pile onto that unfairness by blaming them?

My therapist, choosing to break the silence this time, suggested an exercise. She gave me two wandlike objects to hold in each hand. They were plugged in and would send small vibrations in an alternating manner into my hands. This was supposed to help me relax and focus on the exercise, to bring me more directly into the moment.

"Now, I want you to imagine you are seated at a table with your parents," she said. "Right now. Today. You can ask them about all of this. How do you imagine this conversation going?"

I put myself in that situation and imagined the conversation. I remained silent, playing the conversation out in my head. Several minutes later, I let out a long, slow breath. "I can't fix this," I said simply.

We discussed this conclusion for the rest of our session. I realized that you could put me in a time machine and, even knowing what I now know, send me back to my childhood, and there was no way I could make my family happy during that time period.

This brought me tremendous relief. I had recently moved down to 0.25 milligrams on the clonazepam, and the anxiety had been pretty bad for several days. It drained out of me completely, and I felt at peace, starting from the moment I said those words, "I can't fix this."

I arrived back home in Bellevue late the next day and told my wife, "I think I know what's wrong with me."

Two things could have occurred to me at that point that would have helped me enormously.

First, why exactly did it matter so much that, no matter what I did, I couldn't have fixed my family? What if I could have? Would it have been so bad to go back in time and realize, yeah, that's where I screwed up? I could have done that differently. No guarantees even then, but that would have been the better choice. I could have realized that the way I constructed the "I can't fix this" thing simply fed into my pathological need to be perfect, to never make a mistake that I don't at some point correct. Not "Oh, thank God, I see I did nothing wrong" but the far more mentally healthy approach of "Damn, I messed up, but that's okay. I'm still worthy of love in this world."

Second, from this, I could have thought more deeply about how my success in life impacted my problematic outlook on the unacceptability of my making mistakes.

Yes, those mistakes had still gnawed at me even during the time before my anxiety attack, but I had also kind of white-washed those mistakes. That was the beauty of my election to the state Senate in that huge upset win at the age of twenty-five, and my subsequent professional and personal success in life. Those successes meant that I hadn't really ever made any huge mistakes. Those mistakes had all been necessary to help me succeed. I could live with them as part of some larger grand plan for me in the universe—as long as I kept succeeding by whatever crazy measure of my success I developed in my mind, kept moving relentlessly up this imagined ladder of success. Now, what the hell happens if I stumble on that ladder? I just didn't want to think about that. I repressed it, if you will.

People make mistakes. We all make mistakes. That fact, again, does not make any of us less worthy of love. This is what I still didn't fully appreciate, even after my breakthrough during therapy back in June of 2014.

CHAPTER 13
Hip Pain and Hip Surgeons

T he self-reflection helped, even if it missed the mark slightly. I worked my way down to 0.125 on the clonazepam, kept seeing my therapist, and by mid-July finally believed I saw the light at the end of the tunnel. I felt consistently pretty good—limited anxiety and a feeling that the drug was working its way out of me and leaving my mind much clearer.

Then I had a new problem. The pain started on July 15. My left groin muscle started aching a few hours after a treadmill workout, to the point where lifting my left leg up to walk hurt badly. It didn't bother me that much mentally. I was supposed to stop over-worrying, right? I found it more annoying than anything. My body frequently hurt in a variety of ways—bad back, sore knee, foot pain, and various muscle aches over the years. I always just rode it out, and eventually it at least got back to the point where I was able to do what I needed to do.

"If I was a horse, they would have shot me a long time ago," I said to my staff as I explained why I was going to see the physical therapist (PT) at the House physician's office.

But the pain didn't go away. It got steadily worse. The entire area around my left hip got more and more painful to move when walking. I saw a few different PTs in July and August, but nothing seemed to help. Worst of all, climbing hills, the one thing all my other ailments seemed okay with me doing, became a major trigger for the pain around my left hip.

Meanwhile, I kept working my way down on the clonazepam dosage, but I had stopped seeing my therapist. I wasn't in DC for almost six weeks from the end of July past Labor Day, so it wasn't possible then, and by the time I got back, my physical pain became my focus. I did manage to get completely off the drug by the end of August. The pain got even worse the week after Labor Day. It spread to my upper buttock and lower back. I couldn't sleep on my side because of the hip pain, and I couldn't sleep on my back because of the back pain. I couldn't sleep, period. Anxiety and panic took over. I had no idea what to do, and one of my old, central fears returned—it's the stuff I don't worry about that gets me in trouble. I hadn't worried when this pain first hit. Now look at me. Completely screwed.

Finally, on a day in the last week of September I found myself back in a familiar spot: talking in a fatalistic monotone to yet another doctor, convinced once again that my life was over. This time it was one of the doctors at the House physician's office. I asked about the possibility of getting some serious pain meds— oxycodone or some other opiate. She rejected this, to her credit. Instead, I went back on clonazepam. This devasted me after all I had been through to get off of it, but I didn't think I had a choice. I needed something to relax me enough to get to sleep.

I did consider the possibility that my mental issues had manifested into physical pain. I will have much more to say on this subject later in my story, but at this point I reached the simple conclusion that whatever those issues might be doing to contribute to the level of my pain, there was no way they were the main cause.

The pain, my doctor in DC and I decided, did seem to be coming from my hip. The Seattle/King County area has no shortage of highly respected medical professionals, including orthopedic surgeons who specialize in hips. I asked around, got a few recommendations, and settled on one. Then I got an MRI of both hips and made an appointment to see him. This began a long, painful, frustrating education on how our body's muscular/skeletal/nervous system works, and all the many splendid ways it can fail. I also received a similar education in the quirky world of all those medical professionals who attempt to explain it and treat it.

It seemed simple at first. I sat with the hip surgeon and looked at the images of my hip. "You have impingements on both sides," he said. I had no idea what that meant, but I quickly learned. The hip is a ball and a socket—the ball at the top of

your femur fitting into the socket of your pelvis. An impingement occurs when the parts of that socket don't wrap either
neatly or completely around the ball.

My right hip had never been flexible. I could never cross my
legs by putting my right ankle on top of my left knee while I was
sitting or sit on the floor with my legs crossed underneath me.
Not for as far back as I could remember anyway. But it was my
left hip that hurt. Neither hip had much flexibility, it turned out,
because both were impinged. The exact diagnosis was a femoral
acetabular impingement (FAI).

The hip surgeon then explained that you can live with an
impingement your whole life without any problem. That kind of
depended on what sort of physical activity you did, however. I
walked up hills a lot, and also, in an effort to strengthen my legs
and butt to protect my sore knee and back, I did a particular
leg-press machine quite a bit. I had struggled for years to find
leg exercises that didn't wind up hurting my right knee. Squats,
stairs, and a fair number of leg-press machines didn't work for
me as my knee wound up sore. But then I found one that did.

The surgeon concluded that this exercise routine would aggravate an impingement, which would lead to the development
of bone spurs and tears in the cartilage around the hip—exactly
what had occurred in both my hips as shown on the screen in
front of us. This seemed straightforward to me at the time. Torn
cartilage. Bone spurs. Pain.

I've since learned that our muscular/skeletal/nervous system is a much trickier bastard than that. If you take 100 MRIs of
the shoulders (the only other ball-and-socket joint in our body)
of 100 Major League pitchers, where none of them have suffered

any obvious injury, as much as 50 percent of these shoulders will show damage, at times significant damage, but without any noticeable pain or loss of function. Studies like this have been done. The point is there is not the direct correlation between damage found on an MRI and resulting pain or loss of function one would assume. Some look awful and create no problems. Others have minor tears and big problems. The whole system is interconnected. Other seemingly unrelated parts of the muscular/skeletal/nervous system could be the true cause of the pain.

Ignorant of this reality, I assumed we had found the problem. Now, what should we do about it? Minimally invasive, arthroscopic FAI surgery is a relatively new procedure for the hip developed in the late 1990s and early 2000s. The surgeon goes through a tiny incision and then uses tiny instruments to clear up the cartilage tears and reshape the bone so the ball and the socket fit better. My surgeon told me that without this procedure, I would soon damage my hips to the point where both would have to be replaced.

I asked around, did research on the Internet, and discovered this surgery was not without controversy. Many doubted the necessity of the procedure, arguing that the hip pain that usually led to it could be better treated through physical therapy. A number of websites were dedicated to this argument, complete with a wide variety of stretches and exercises designed to better cure the problem without having a surgeon poke a hole in you and mess around inside your hip joint, shaving away at bone. I could not, however, even begin to do most of these exercises and stretches. My knee pain and back pain had limited me for years. Now, the pain in my hips, butt, and groin limited me even more. I tried the few exercises I thought might be okay, but no luck. The pain got worse.

One other trend stood out in what people had to say about hip surgery. They tended to have a more positive view of recovery from total hip replacement (THR) than recovery from FAI surgery. Both had horror stories along with rave reviews to be sure, but the overall picture left the distinct impression of an easier road coming back from THR.

One big aspect of THR did concern me, however. The material I read said that for eight to twelve weeks after the surgery, you had to be very careful not to bend your hip past ninety degrees. If you did, the new metallic ball might pop out of the new metallic socket. Yikes. How can one live for that long without, essentially, ever bending over? They gave instructions, but they seemed really complicated. And if you messed up? Well, then you're writhing around on the floor in blinding agony.

I found salvation on this issue in the form of "minimally invasive" anterior THR. This relatively new procedure used an incision on the front of the hip instead of the standard posterior approach. It would be idiotic to call any surgery to totally replace your hip joint "minimally invasive," but the anterior approach eliminated the need, in recovery, to avoid bending the hip past ninety degrees. Better yet, two of the most experienced orthopedic surgeons in anterior THR worked at the University of Washington Medical Center.

Why not just go straight to replacement? FAI might not work, from what I read, then you had to get the hip replaced anyway. Maybe FAI would only buy me a few years even if it did work. I set an appointment with one of the UW surgeons.

I arrived at that appointment in very bad shape. The pain kept getting worse. Worry was my constant companion as I battled to figure out how to keep my life from falling apart. The flights back and forth to DC were brutal, and I found it harder and harder to do the minimum amount necessary at work and at home. I stood in line, waiting to check in for my appointment with my left hip/groin/buttock and my right foot aching so badly I wasn't sure how long I could remain standing. But sitting was actually worse—all that pressure going right down on my hip, butt, and lower back.

The nurse checked my vitals once I got checked in and shown to an examination room. My resting pulse rate was 112. Normally, if I could even count anything as having ever been normal by this point, it was around 60.

The doctor, when he arrived, focused on my anxiety. He saw the vitals and the medications I had listed I was taking. I was not my normal articulate self as I tried to explain my history with anxiety. Plus, it felt to me like he was scolding me. I felt mildly annoyed at this but also ashamed. I wasn't calm and coherent enough to even handle this "meeting" properly. And you know me when I think I'm messing up. Eventually, we focused on my hip pain and the MRIs, but the surgeon still kept on about how anxiety could cause physical pain. It was a growing area of study in the medical profession, he told me.

"I just don't believe this is all in my head," I said. He offered some explanation about how it wasn't technically correct to describe psychosomatic pain as being "all in your head." I blew past that. "I mean. Look at those MRIs. The bone spurs, torn cartilage."

"I've seen worse," he responded. *Okay, I thought. Good for you. I'm not trying to win a contest here.* "I'm not convinced that even the physical portion of your pain is coming from your hip," he continued.

He did not offer an alternative location, however. I told him about my exercise routine, and he suggested that might be part of the problem. "Not good, exercises for the hip," he explained. *But you just said the pain wasn't coming from my hip,* I thought but did not say, not wanting to be argumentative.

"You should try deep-water running," he said. I swear to God I'm not making this up. That's what he said. "Much easier on the joints."

Again, words failed me, but not long after I left I thought, *It hurts for me to walk, jackass. I can't exactly deep-water run through the airport or from my office over to the Capitol for votes.*

Finally, this surgeon explained that FAI surgery was a terrible idea. He dismissed it as quackery that couldn't possibly help.

I believed in God. I believed He had a plan for me. I looked for signs, always trusting that He would send me in the right direction, even if that trust had frayed somewhat at this point. This belief set served me poorly in this process. I was strung out, unable to think clearly. Surely, God would guide me to the right decision. That's how I felt when I set the appointment with the UW surgeon. It felt right. Bite the bullet. Get the THR. Anterior for a quicker recovery.

Then this guy, metaphorically, took out a .357 Magnum and blew God's head off as I sat and watched.

The original orthopedic surgeon I had seen, turns out, had once worked with the other one. Small world. "That guy just hates FAI because he never figured out how to do it," he explained when I went back to him after my failed flirtation with anterior THR. My less confrontational orthopedic surgeon also offered his thoughts on FAI versus THR. "Ultimately, it's up to you," he said. "I do both." He did the posterior version only, however, and was very good at it from all reports. "Personally, I think FAI will be best for you," he continued. "The original parts usually work better than replacements."

I took his advice. FAI surgery on my left hip it was, set for October 31, 2014.

CHAPTER 14
The Struggle Is Real

The recovery did not go well.

I focused, at first, on what seemed like strict instructions from my surgeon on what I needed to do in that recovery. Very limited activity for the first six weeks, being especially careful not to take my normal stride. I had to take very short strides so as not to aggravate the surgically repaired hip. Then a slowly increasing set of exercises and stretches. But these "strict" instructions kept changing.

I did not see the surgeon again. My follow-up appointments were with various assistants and came every couple of weeks.

These assistants gave very different answers on what I should be doing. The time period for inactivity changed as did the exercises and stretches. Eventually, they sent me to a physical therapist they worked with, and he showed me another series of stretches and exercises. The precise rhyme or reason to these eluded me, and my pain only reduced slightly.

Orthopedic surgeon number one did turn out to be right about one thing—left to its own devices, my right hip quickly failed. The pain in that hip drove me back to the world of orthopedic surgery. Dissatisfied with my experience with surgeon number one, and hoping to never again even see potential surgeon number two, I asked around for another recommendation and found a group of orthopedic surgeons operating in connection with Swedish Hospital. I got another MRI and surgeons number three and four—they worked together—declared my right hip trashed and in need of replacement.

I got this surgery in March of 2015—an anterior THR. The good news? The new metallic ball never popped out of the new metallic socket.

I spent the rest of that year desperately trying to recover from both of these surgeries. Oh, and I kept popping clonazepam to try to ward off the worst of the anxiety.

Pain medication figured prominently in this effort, as did a seemingly endless string of physical therapists, massage therapists, personal trainers, and doctors specializing in pain management. And a couple of podiatrists. Remember how I said, when I string-cited the different types of healthcare professionals I cycled through, I might not even be remembering some of them? I forgot the podiatrists. A couple of them misdiagnosed my foot problems three or four times.

The pain medication became a big deal. I took oxycodone after both of the surgeries and got to experience the joy of titrating off of this drug. I also kept a stash even after the times I had "stopped" taking it, for those days when I couldn't take the pain anymore. I took 2,000 milligrams of Tylenol and 200 milligrams of Celebrex every day, the entire time. I was also introduced to drugs called gabapentin, tramadol, and amitriptyline, which I cycled on and off of depending on a combination of how much I thought they were helping, how badly I thought I needed the help, and how freaked out I was about the possibility of dependence/side effects.

I could explain a lot about both the decisions by various doctors and me to take each of these drugs, and precisely how each impacted me, but that would be longer than it would be illuminating. Suffice to say it was an epic battle. Did some of these drugs, at different times, help me to simply keep going? Absolutely. Were they ever a long-term solution? Absolutely not.

The physical therapy focused on an endless analysis of what hurt, what might be causing it, and what might I do to relieve that hurt. Here it suffices to say that I don't think much of the physical therapy profession or the various other medical professionals professing to focus on dealing with pain. I learned the details of the errors of their ways only later, but at the time, I kept thinking the next one I saw would have the answers to my problems. If I just found the right stretch, the right exercise to get the right muscles stronger, the right pressure point to make the muscle work properly.

Why did I see so many different people? Three reasons. First, I wasn't getting better. I had to keep searching. Second, I'm a bit obsessive about never giving up and searching relentlessly until I find the right answer. Third, everybody knows "a guy." People could see how much pain I was in as I went about my life, and a fair number of them had some experience or knew somebody who had some experience with pain. "Congressman, you have to see this PT I worked with last year after my skiing accident. He's the best."

How did I keep going during this period? How did I even begin to meet all of those responsibilities I listed earlier? For my job. To my family. Part of the answer reminds me of what a couple of good friends of mine told me after their second child turned out to be twins, born eighteen months after their first child. "We've got seven months of our lives we really just don't remember," they both agreed. "It's all just a blur." Much of this period in my life is a blur as well, but I also had a lot of help—my staff and wife most prominently. I didn't do as much as I had done before, and they picked up that slack. And I lived with the pain and anxiety as I traveled back and forth to DC and did the meetings I had to do. No way I was as productive as I was before—I did fewer meetings, attended fewer events, and so forth. But I was productive enough, and again, my wife and my staff helped me out a ton.

The hardest part was deciding what to do day in and day out. Can I do that meeting? Can I drive my son to soccer practice? Go out to dinner with the family? Keep sitting in this meeting for another five minutes? Ten? Should I just take another oxycodone or clonazepam and lay in bed for the rest of the day?

Should I ask someone on my staff to go down to the cafeteria and get me my lunch?

I hated asking for help even before all of this, and now I had to worry if asking for help was one more piece of straw on the back of the idea that I was ever going to get better. And I wondered how long people would be willing to keep helping me. I was hardwired to believe that, at the end of the day, I was on my own. People leave. Or die. That's what they do. But now, I couldn't even begin to be on my own. I needed so much help.

I really hated the whole situation.

CHAPTER 15
Chronic
Pain Management

'll return to this point later in greater detail, but here I will give a
quick, top-level assessment of the flaws and inherent limitations
in our current approach to pain management.

First, remember the incredible complexity of the human
body. This isn't easy. A given patient walks in complaining of
pain, it could be a lot of different things.

Second, even as one of these pain professionals looks for a
solution, there is the possibility of something really bad being

wrong. So, if a given course of action doesn't work, it might just be because of something that can't be entirely fixed. It's like looking for something in the closet when you really don't believe it's there. You won't look as thoroughly because you don't quite believe you will find it even if you do. Okay, we tried a few exercises, and the pain is still there. Maybe your hip is shot. Maybe you have bursitis that won't go away. Maybe your sacrum is screwed up. Maybe you have rheumatoid arthritis. Or any one of a dozen different problems for which the best we can do is manage the pain.

I actually got "diagnosed" as having a cracked sesamoid bone in my right foot at one point. I didn't, but the pain had to be coming from somewhere, right? Otherwise, why weren't all those rehab stretches and exercises the PTs were giving me working? And there really isn't a lot you can do about a cracked sesamoid bone except try to stay off your feet and hope it heals.

Third, very few people and very few healthcare professionals possess the relentless, focused, intellectual rigor to do battle with these complexities. As I explained in the opening chapter, it's not how our healthcare system is set up.

Fourth, and this is crucial to understand, the human body isn't just complex; it's the most magnificent machine ever conceived. It has a power to heal itself that is beyond amazing. Somehow, my body managed to function reasonably well for over thirty years after I mistakenly decided I couldn't use my right knee as it was intended to be used. An amazing healing machine, our bodies.

So, you have bad pain, and you go see a physical therapist. You get examined. Do a few weeks of sessions and adopt some new exercises or stretches. And, wow, you feel better! That therapist is a genius. Except, probably not. Your body probably just did a combination of healing and developing work-arounds—making greater use of muscles not necessarily intended for a given movement because of the pain in the muscles the body was supposed to be using for that movement—to reduce your pain. But the PT thinks what he did made the difference, so he keeps doing it on other patients.

And that's the rub. The human body has an amazing capacity to heal itself. Until it doesn't. Then you need to really think about what's wrong, not just pull a few exercises and stretches off of YouTube videos.

Fifth, the time thing. The quick solution is what both the doctor and the patient want. Take a few pills. Do a few exercises. All good; back to work. The pills are a huge problem. A ton of fixable conditions go unresolved, and a ton of new, often worse, conditions get created because so many doctors in this country pass out pain meds like some kind of Walter White Pez dispensers. They are even worse on the mental health side, passing out anti-anxiety and antidepressant meds.

I fell deep into the pit of all these things in 2015. I could not climb stairs at all. I live in a two-story house with all the bedrooms upstairs. I kept the crutches from my surgeries and used one every time I had to go upstairs—one arm on the crutch, the opposite hand using the railing as I propelled myself upward. Sitting was excruciating unless I took the more aggressive pain meds. The pain had some favorite spots—my left hip, right hamstring, right foot. But it got creative, too. Lower back, shoulders. Muscle cramps that hit both of my feet, my abductors. My right quad took to spasming when I first got out of bed in the morning to the point where I almost collapsed until I got a few steps under me.

I could walk but not for very long, and going up the slightest hill set off a ton of pain. I had used a scooter briefly after my FAI surgery, to get around at the Capitol, but as sitting became more painful than walking, that ceased to be an option. Nonetheless, I felt compelled to try to keep moving when I could and would take short walks, just circling my floor in the Rayburn House Office Building back in DC or walking back and forth on the short dead-end street where I lived back in Bellevue when I was home. We lived in a small, fifty-four-home development, but I did not dare venture into any of the other cul-de-sacs in our neighborhood because that involved hills. I tried to force myself to take these walks, but there were days when I barely moved off the couch or my bed.

I did what exercises I could and worked with all those healthcare providers who tried to help me. My right hip seemed to be improving slightly, but my left seemed stubbornly stuck in pain. Like swinging a rusty gate, I took to describing it.

My anxiety remained firmly in place, and I saw several new therapists, focusing on those specializing in "pain management" at this point. None helped.

CHAPTER 16
I Hate Myself

ometime in the fall of 2015, I was seeing a medical doctor at UW specializing in muscular/skeletal problems when he suggested a psychologist he knew who, once again, specialized in chronic pain. The UW doctor and I had been discussing, to no useful conclusion, how my anxiety might be contributing to my physical pain. He, unlike his orthopedic surgeon UW colleague, did not dismiss the physical side but did understand that anxiety could contribute to physical pain.

I agreed to give the psychologist a try. I don't remember why exactly. I didn't see everybody somebody suggested to me. That would have been impossible. But this guy did take insurance.

My insurance for some reason only charged a fifteen-dollar co-pay for a one-hour visit. Winner, winner, chicken dinner as they say. It was almost like saving money after some of my more expensive experiments with people or programs that might help me.

This guy did require me to fill out the longest questionnaire I had ever seen. This annoyed me. I spent most of my time lying down at this point, and you can't effectively fill out a questionnaire in that position, so I had to sit, painfully as always, to fill the damn thing out.

I went to my first session and sat down, again, painfully, across from him in his office. No, therapists don't really have couches, at least none of the ones I ever saw did. I don't think we said much more than "Hello" before he said, glancing through my questionnaire, "You don't think you have the right to exist." I don't remember if I bowed my head slightly or rolled my eyes or rubbed my forehead with my hand or closed my eyes completely in aggravation. But I was thinking it. *Great. Another waste of my time.* What the hell did that even mean?

He did try to explain as we discussed my history and issues for the rest of the hour. Something about me believing that I was unworthy of love, that I felt like a failure not deserving of the respect of others. I argued this point. Come on, I've had people call me arrogant more than once in my life. I'm successful professionally. Good at my job.

"You think that's what gives you worth as a human being? How good you are at your job? That's where you find your self-worth?"

I could easily sense that the correct answer to this question in this guy's mind was, no. But, come on. *Of course, that's where I got my sense of self-worth. Where else was there?* "Oh, well, I think I'm a good father and husband," I added as I thought about the question more. "I'm a decent person. Kind to others, that kind of thing."

"You get your self-worth from your deeds. Your accomplishments."

Again, duh. I'm worthy because of what I do. Isn't that just the way it is?

No, he told me. That's not the way it is.

I fought him on this issue, and several others, for over three years. I'm stubborn.

One thought did occur to me as I drove home from that first session with my latest therapist. It was what I said to myself every single morning when I first woke up, starting at some point not long after my anxiety and pain overwhelmed me.

"I hate myself."

That's what I said—and kept saying for a long time after this initial therapy session. I said other things as well.

"I hate my life."

"Why, God? Why would you do this to me?"

"I'm so scared."

I had a whole series of fatalistic, negative, pleading, angry things that I both thought and said out loud on a regular basis.

But "I hate myself"? That seemed a little harsh as I thought about it.

CHAPTER 17
One More Hip Surgery

The "Why do I keep saying, 'I hate myself'" revelation did not immediately lead to any kind of breakthrough. I kept seeing the guy but without much hope of significant progress and a somewhat disagreeable take on his idea that I didn't think I had a right to exist. Again, what did that even mean?

Meanwhile, I kept wondering, *Could some new physical therapist or pain management doctor finally give me the key to getting better? Could some slightly different take from one of the ones I had already been seeing make that happen?* Or was there something more fundamentally wrong with me that required a more invasive solution, like another surgery? Maybe it was anxiety induced. Maybe the mental health therapy was the key.

It was like a treasure hunt. I kept searching all over my mental and physical house with constant desperation, never quite convinced that I was looking in the right spot.

My muscular/skeletal doctor and I came back to my left hip—the rusty gate as I called it. I never really believed in the FAI surgery. Now that left hip wasn't getting better. Why not just get it replaced, make sure my hips at least are functioning, commit to rehab at that point, and go from there?

We had discovered all manner of other problems with my body by this point. Things that should have made me more skeptical about another major surgery being my best approach. My lower spine was severely bent to the right. No scoliosis. More like a straight pipe that just got bent starting about three-quarters of the way down. My pelvis was also badly rotated forward on the left. I had no reflexes in my right heel, and very limited flexibility throughout my entire lower body. I had poked around at all of this with the doctor and a bunch of massage and physical therapists, learning about muscles and parts of my body I never knew existed—hip flexors, the sacrum, the psoas, SI joints, and my personal favorite, the ischial tuberosity. But, as the saying goes, no joy. I still wasn't getting better.

Oddly, surgery had a positive allure to me. First, it held the promise of the big fix. Ah, that was it all along. Two fully functioning artificial hips and presto, I'm able to get my strength and flexibility back. Second, I could take drugs for a few weeks without the angst. Everybody takes opiates after hip replacement, after all. Third, it would buy me a brief period of peace, a solid excuse for doing nothing but taking pain meds and recuperating for at least a while. I recognize the illogic of this outlook. I obviously knew at this point that recovery from surgery was never easy, and what about the anxiety/difficulty of eventually coming off of those pain meds? But the allure of that above-described brief period of peace had a powerful attraction for me by this time that defied such logic.

I have no way to ever know for sure if I needed to replace my left hip, but that's what I decided to do. So, back into the world of orthopedic surgeons. I had no shortage of options at this point, given my prior experience, and all the people I now knew who had gone through hip replacement surgery. It's like when you buy a new car. Suddenly you see the make and model you bought everywhere. Your senses tune into this aspect of the world.

I rejected my prior surgeons, still wanting the anterior approach, and not thrilled with the results and follow-up from the ones who replaced my right hip. I got a hematoma from that surgery—internal damage to a blood vessel that releases blood inside your body—my hip, in this case. Doesn't kill you like it would if it happened in your brain or other sensitive organs, but it does prolong recovery and give you nasty bruising all the way down your leg as the blood drains according to the law of gravity.

My follow-up appointments with those guys also didn't go well. I honestly don't know why orthopedic surgeons do follow-up appointments. Their job is done. They know how to cut and replace—very specialized skills—but they know very little about recovery. Insurance does, however, cover two or three follow-up appointments, so there you are. If the surgery went well, it's all smiles and high fives. Not much to be done. If it doesn't go well or if for some reason the patient is not recovering as hoped, well, then—still not much to be done. Once again in the sucks-to-be-you category, but what is the surgeon supposed to do about it?

Then there was the recall issue. I didn't focus a lot on precisely what kind of metallic joint they were putting in me. He's the surgeon, right? These surgeons do hundreds of these things, and joint replacement seemed to be a very well-developed and successful operation. Surely, they aren't going to put something in me that creates problems. Skipping too many of the details, a relatively new type of joint involving two bend points was being recalled.

Think about that for a second. Not exactly like recalling lawn darts. Uh, yeah, those parts we stuck in your body through that large slice in your flesh? The things making your leg move at this point? We're going to need those back.

Come to find out my surgeons didn't use the more widely accepted single-jointed ceramic ball and titanium socket artificial hip on me. They used a double-jointed one. Yes, I should have paid more attention to this when they told me about it before my surgery, but, remember, I was just ever so slightly freaked out at that time.

I called my surgeon's assistant to inquire about this issue. She was pretty tired of me by this point. I kept having questions about why I was still in so much pain long after the surgery, and remember, her office isn't getting paid to talk to me on the phone after the surgery is done.

"Don't worry," she told me. "Your type of hip joint hasn't been recalled yet."

Again, I'm not making this up. She said, "Yet." I expressed some level of discomfort with the word, but she dismissed me, telling me to set an appointment if I had any questions for the doctor.

The first new option I chose to seek out told me he could not be sure my pain was coming from that left hip. Very smart guy, and frankly probably the best orthopedic surgeon I talked to throughout this process. He had a sterling reputation, and I had first met him years before in my professional capacity. He didn't lecture me about anxiety or deep-water running; he just offered his honest professional opinion that, from what he saw on my MRI and X-rays, THR wasn't warranted. I should have accepted that answer, but I cycled through a few more options before finding one who recommended the surgery. He, too, had a great reputation. I knew a guy, of course, who had gotten a THR from this doctor, and the guy raved about it.

Was this latest orthopedic surgeon probably a little too willing to do the surgery just because he makes his living getting paid to do these surgeries? Like the magic eight ball says, all signs point to yes. But I was desperate. I wanted to believe this was the solution.

Orthopedic surgeons, I have come to believe, should be like field-goal kickers—highly skilled professionals who never actually make the ultimate decision on when they perform that skill. Sure, they should be consulted on the decision, like, *How's the leg feeling today, Joey? You think you got a fifty-five-yarder in you?* But, given inherent biases, these surgeons should simply be called in by other doctors who have determined the surgery is needed. The orthopedic surgeon does the job, and that's it. No pointless follow-up appointments. The surgeon's job is done. Stick to what you know, like they say in that song from *High School Musical.*

I got my left hip replaced in early February of 2016. The surgeon did a fine job. No hematoma. No possibility of him needing to ask me for the new joint back. I did not, however, get better. I wasn't in great shape to begin with, and surgeries are no walk in the park in the best of circumstances. The muscles in my lower body atrophied to the truly scary point where I didn't want to even look at them.

My son sent me an email at some point, in between my two THR surgeries. He shares my love of sports, and from the time he could walk, we played together—throwing a ball back and forth, working up to Nerf basketball, real basketball, throwing a football in our yard. He became a soccer player at the age of four and kept playing right through high school at a fairly high level. We spent more time on more different fields than I can remember kicking the ball back and forth and having penalty-kick and other shooting contests. He's a striker, and watching him score goals over the course of his childhood will always be one of the greatest joys I have experienced in life.

We had not been out to a field together since a few months before my first hip surgery in 2014. He was eleven at that point. His email told me that he knew I was going to get better and that he couldn't wait to get back out on the field and kick the soccer ball with me.

I kept the email. It broke my heart every time I read it. I just couldn't picture the path back to that ever happening.

CHAPTER 18

He's Not Dead;
He's Mostly Dead

A pril 2016. *Weekend at Bernie's.* That's what I took to calling it. My team and I had to act like I wasn't dead. Just like the two friends had to do with the Bernie character in that ridiculous but oddly successful absurdist comedy. They actually made a sequel. You know, he's still dead. How funny is that?

Two chief forcing mechanisms pushed me forward and out of bed that April. First, one of those rumors about somebody running against me turned into an actual fact. I faced possibly legitimate opposition in my campaign for reelection that year. Who would hire someone who could barely get out of bed if I lost my job? I viewed the possibility of not being reelected as an existential threat under the circumstances. Second, the Armed Services Committee, of which I was still the ranking Democrat, had set the annual markup of the defense bill for the end of the month. The committee usually does only one bill a year, but it is the defense budget, a roughly 2,000-page, $700-billion-plus piece of legislation. The committee marks it up each year in a meeting that lasts all day and, often, well into the next morning. The ranking member leads his party in this effort, and my presence was therefore pretty much required.

I was beyond scared with no clue how I would meet either of these challenges. I could barely get out of bed and feed myself at that point. But I decided on a simple approach. Survive. Don't give up. Whine and cry all you want, be as scared as you want, as angry as you want, as frustrated as you want. But survive. Don't give up.

I made the flight back to DC and found a way to stay back there for the three weeks leading up to the markup, figuring it wise to avoid as many cross-country flights as I could. Drugs figured prominently in this survival plan: clonazepam to be sure, the consistent doses of Tylenol and Celebrex, amitriptyline (also a consistent dose by then), gabapentin from time to time, and a much bigger emphasis on tramadol. I had decided to pass on oxycodone, going with the tramadol as my opiate of choice.

I had a bed in my office at that point with a closet large enough to store it in during the day. I lay down on that bed in that closet whenever I could, and, on the day of the mark-up, my staff moved the bed down into a small room just off the committee room so I could take breaks and use it to lie down and reduce the pain before returning to the committee room as needed. The markup lasted until four-thirty in the morning, but I made it. I survived. I didn't give up.

Back home in the district, my staff would come by my house, I would pull myself off of my couch, get out to the car, deposit myself in the passenger seat, make it through as many meetings and campaign events as I had to/could, acting like I wasn't scared to death and on the brink of collapse, then flop back into the car for the return home, where I went back inside and lay down again.

Weekend at Bernie's. A very long weekend as it happened.

You may be wondering at this point what all the various people who would come into contact with me during all of this thought about my situation. Clearly, a huge part of this I don't know. You'd have to ask them. I liked to think that I put on a brave face, and most people, preoccupied in their own worlds, didn't notice anything amiss. But I'm pretty sure that's not the case.

I wound up waiting for an elevator once, sometime late in 2016, in the Rayburn House Office Building next to Congressman Mike Turner, a Republican from Ohio and a senior member of the House Armed Services Committee. Mike and I had done battle quite often over the years, usually in a good-natured way, but not always. We both had an intensity about how we advocated for and defended our positions on issues. We got along fine, however.

"Adam," he said as I stood hoping the elevator would hurry up so I could get back to my office and lie down. "I really admire you." I gave him a raised eyebrow look in response. "Everybody can see how much pain you are in. Sitting in committee. Walking. And you keep doing the job. It's impressive."

So, yeah, people probably did notice far more than I realized at the time.

More than a few of my staff became important confidants in the process, as did several close friends. My staff drove me around and/or had to work with me on that fun-filled and constant effort of deciding what I could and could not do. I talked openly with them about the struggle, usually going for matter-of-fact gallows humor, but also being more desperately fatalistic at times.

I get fairly emotional when I think back on all the people who helped me during this period. They put the lie to my misguided notion that I was all alone in this world. I will never forget the kindness and support they all gave me.

For the rest of 2016, through 2017, and into 2018, I dove back into the world of physical therapy, massage, and personal trainers, still searching for the answer. Based on the recommendations of a few people (everybody knows a guy, remember), I became focused on a thing called myofascial release. This involved sessions with a therapist who aggressively massaged key muscles—aggressive to the point of being quite painful—and epic amounts of stretching.

Myofascial release therapists were—say it with me—not covered by insurance. I also bought a very large, exhaustive book called *Becoming a Supple Leopard,* which contained more stretches and other means of forcing flexibility into your muscles than I could have imagined possible. A lacrosse ball figured prominently. I followed the instructions, placing the small, hard ball under various parts of my body, then putting my body weight on top of the ball so pressure could be applied directly to a given muscle. It hurt in the moment. How much it helped in the long run is highly debatable.

This all contains the germ of a very important idea—muscles need to be "activated" before strength and flexibility can truly be achieved. Now, exactly how to do that requires a bit more subtlety and knowledge of how muscles work than the brute force and relentless stretching contained in myofascial release, but what the hell did I know at this point? I found the time to see the therapists and do the stretching. I didn't get much better, but I kept moving forward. I also decided that I needed a better analogy. Bernie is, after all, dead. No coming back from that, the sequel notwithstanding.

I went with *The Princess Bride.* He's not dead; he's mostly dead. Sure, Wesley's stretched out on the bed holding a sword and unable to move, but he will get better. Question is, will he get better in time to stop the guy coming at him from killing him? Or, if not, can he bluff the guy into thinking he's stronger than he appears?

I won reelection by a comfortable margin and moved into 2017 surviving but certainly not thriving.

More therapists followed. Personal trainers as well. I analyzed every stretch, every exercise, refining what I did on a constant basis. I discovered "dry needling," a procedure where the therapist sticks a three- or four-inch needle deep into whatever muscle you are trying to stimulate. A variation on the myofascial release muscle-activation idea. My back gave out several times, leaving me in even more crippling pain, and various other muscles and joints continued their assault on me, even as I did get just a little stronger and more flexible. I still couldn't climb stairs, still used the crutch every time I had to go upstairs at home. I got on and off tramadol while keeping the other drugs mostly constant. Needless to say, my travels around the country and around the world had ceased. I made it back and forth to DC because I had no choice. I took a seat cushion with me everywhere. The Miracle Bamboo Cushion. There's no bamboo involved, so I'm not sure about the name, but I highly recommend the cushion. Even with it, sitting was still painful as all hell. I went to my son's soccer games when they weren't so far away as to require an overnight stay somewhere. I kept doing my job as best as I could.

Like I said, it's all kind of a blur past a certain point.

I still woke up every morning, dreading having to get out of bed and saying "I hate myself."

CHAPTER 19
Psychotherapy

The aim of psychotherapy is not to correct the past. It is to help the patient to confront his own history and to grieve over it. There is a lot to unpack in these two sentences, but I have come to believe that they are crucial to the mental health of us as individuals and for all of us as a society. The only thing I would add is that the same type of analysis that goes into psychotherapy's explorations of a patient's past can also apply to issues facing a patient in the present.

We all have a past: things we lived through a long time ago or maybe just yesterday. We all have regrets: things we did in that past that we feel some level of guilt over and things we feel we never properly atoned for, so the guilt nags at us. We also all have anger over things that have happened to us in our past: things for which we feel we never received a proper apology, adequate justice, or compensation. And things happened to us in that past that, for one reason or another, we let go by without taking the time to truly grieve for something we lost or something that hurt us far more deeply than we realized at the time.

My story is unique in its own way, as all of our stories are, but my story is not unusual. It is not something far outside the norm of human experience, to be looked at as some kind of *Ripley's Believe It or Not* moment.

Again, we all have a past. We all have guilt, anger, and regrets. We all have unresolved issues in our past. The better we learn how to deal with those, the better for all of us.

There is, as with all things, a balance to be struck here—in two areas in particular.

First, focusing on our past so we can best deal with it should not slip into relentless self-importance/navel-gazing. I read somewhere that much of the effort to adequately address the issues in our lives requires a "healthy narcissism." It is important for we humans to, at an early age, develop a firm idea of who we are—a healthy sense of self-love and self-worth. But this does not mean that we should focus on ourselves to the exclusion of all others in the world. There is also such a thing as an unhealthy narcissism. Good to talk to friends, loved ones, and where necessary, trained therapists about issues in your life. Not good to become trapped in an endless loop of constantly talking about every little thing you have found troubling in your life.

Second, we should not let past issues overly debilitate us in the present. Resilience should be one of the purposes of psychotherapy, not helpless dependency. Those past issues cannot come to so dominate our outlook that they become a be-all and end-all excuse for everything. Like "I talked to my therapist this week about how upset I was that my parents wouldn't get me a dog when I was child. It was very upsetting. The trauma from this disappointment and the invalidation of my feelings means that I can't possibly be expected to go to work today, or maybe even for the rest of the month."

I think these two things are why a lot of people reject the entire concept of psychotherapy. They roll their eyes at somebody going on and on about some childhood trauma, and then arguing that society has to take care of them because this trauma has rendered them incapable of caring for themselves. But, again, there is a balance here. Honestly addressing past issues that are causing potentially debilitating levels of anger, guilt, anxiety, and depression is a good thing. People who don't do that are often less productive than they could be in the here and now.

My latest psychologist and I, throughout 2017 and into 2018, dove into my issues, past and present. I had a lot of guilt, anger, and regret, both about my past and about my present circumstances. I still didn't understand exactly how the entire process worked, however. I thought I got the unresolved issue thing. I had pain in my childhood and had suppressed at least some of it. I needed to talk about that with a therapist so I could resolve it. We talked about it, but the anxiety and the physical pain remained.

It was, I believe, in retrospect, a matter of two big issues—one I understood only too well and one I didn't understand at all—and a few other smaller issues we kept nibbling away at but that ultimately could not really get me there unless the two big ones got addressed. The big one I understood was the enormity and complexity of the challenge I was facing—a toxic mix of drugs, anxiety, and physical pain. The sheer size of the problem overwhelmed my traditional efforts to manage anxiety—CBT being one big example.

My new therapist tried a much more detailed and aggressive approach to CBT than I had previously experienced. CBT was also a good example of one of the smaller issues I did need to work on, even if it was not enough to ultimately get me where I wanted to go. I like the phrase "necessary but not sufficient" to describe things like this. CBT, in theory, could help because, while we had to work on the bigger issues, I also had to deal with the short-term challenges in my life while those bigger issues remained unresolved.

We would start with something specific that was making me anxious—the coming holidays, for example. My family always went to Portland, Oregon, where my wife's family lived, for both Thanksgiving and Christmas. This meant more than a four-hour drive in bad traffic. This was even worse than an airplane flight for my pain because I couldn't get up and move around at all. It also meant being in the 2,400-square-foot, hundred-year-old house my wife's parents lived in for several days with the roughly dozen members of her family. Not all would be there all the time, but they all lived nearby and several had children younger than my own.

I needed space to lie down and space to do my stretching routine. I also had to climb the stairs in their two-story house from time to time. Should I bring my crutch? How exactly do I explain to all my in-laws, who were only vaguely aware of my challenges, why I'm using a crutch to climb up a short flight of stairs? Why can't I sit for very long? Why am I disappearing upstairs to find a bed so I can lie down?

We started on the CBT process with the basic question, "On a scale of one to ten, how anxious are you about the trip to your in-laws in Portland for Thanksgiving?"

I grew to hate this question, "On a scale of one to ten . . . ?" I dealt with it on both my pain and my anxiety. The honest answer? I don't know. What should I compare it to, exactly? I'm freaked out, and I'm in pain. Is it a five? A six? What's the quantitative difference there?

My misgivings notwithstanding, the idea was to find ways to bring that number on my level of anxiety down. How? By planning ways to address the issues. If I brought my crutch so I didn't have to worry about the stairs, would that reduce my anxiety? If I made sure I had a cushioned, comfortable chair to sit in, what's the number now? If we plan stops along the way on the drive so I can get out and move around, will that put me more at ease?

I did understand this process. It was, at the end of the day, basically the same thing I had been doing all my life—making to-do lists and planning how to address the challenges in my life. Organization does help reduce anxiety. It gives you greater confidence you will successfully address the things you are

worried about and have a better chance of accomplishing what
you want to accomplish.

But none of this small-bore, how-do-I-survive-Thanksgiving-
with-my-in-laws stuff addressed the constant threat pounding in
my brain from the drugs, anxiety, and pain. I found it equivalent
to a situation where I was standing somewhere with a homicidal
maniac coming at me with a machete, and I was working on a to-
do list to figure out how to make sure I balanced my schedule to
get the grocery shopping done, make it to my daughter's dance
recital, and still return the five phone calls I needed to return.

The drugs remained a double-edged sword—can't live with
them, terrified to try to live without them.

My therapist felt strongly that anti-anxiety and antidepression drugs were way overused in the treatment of mental
health. He told me about a mental health facility in New York
City he went to work at in the 1970s. When he arrived, the facility had every patient on some kind of medication. He asked
why. They need it, came the response. How do you know? No
good response came to that question, so they took every patient
slowly and carefully off of their meds. Ninety percent were either better off or no worse off without the medication.

I knew by this point the difficulty of titrating off of clonazepam, gabapentin, amitriptyline, and tramadol. I had come off
of all of them at least once. I could hope that my anxiety by now
was a result of having built up a tolerance to these drugs and
that if I could just get through the tough titration battle, then
I could knock off two of my three very large problems—drugs
and anxiety. But I also knew that my anxiety had existed before

I started taking any of these drugs. What was different now? CBT? Psychotherapy? Unearthing repressed emotions through psychotherapy? I simply didn't trust I had somehow resolved whatever issues I had and could live a drug-free and anxiety-free life.

My therapist didn't pressure me to get off of the drugs. He worked to get me to the point where I could safely accomplish that goal. But I knew I had to get there. Whatever demons I had inside me had stayed buried for most of my life, but they were out now, and my efforts to drug them into submission had failed.

I also agreed with my therapist's fundamental premise on mental health and the impact of medications on mental health. We have the capacity to heal. Our brains have that capacity to heal as well, with proper treatment. But if you drug the brain, you are often interfering with that healing process. Why then are so many people in our country taking so many prescription drugs for depression and anxiety? Part of it is the patient's desire for a quick fix, just like in my case. Part of it is a relatively small number of people who probably do need the drugs to function.

But a much bigger part is all the money to be made by convincing doctors to prescribe, and patients to take, these drugs. Society has focused a great deal on the outrageous cost of certain prescription medications, and rightly so. But the overutilization of many of these drugs, driven by a healthcare and drug industry focused more on making money than on positive results for patients is every little bit as evil and devastating to our society.

I wanted off the drugs. CBT was not getting me there on its own. Thus, I had to dive further into my potentially repressed memories, unresolved issues from my past and present, and that basic sense of self-worth concept my therapist had hit me with the very first time we spoke.

We spent time going back and discussing the details of my childhood. What might I be repressing?

But the concept does not always play out in a straightforward manner. I've seen the movies and read the books where the main character, or real-life person in nonfiction accounts, suddenly and shockingly remembers incidents of abuse, or where they had always remembered the abuse but are only now finally addressing it. They let the steam off this way. They understand their history and grieve for what they have lost. But why does this help exactly? Why does this release them from their anxiety or depression?

This would be the second big issue I needed to confront, the one I didn't understand for a long time. Mental health depends on a basic, fundamental sense of self-worth—a healthy narcissism. Mentally healthy people develop that very early in life and are able to maintain it throughout their lives. It comes primarily from having loving, reasonably stable parents or caregivers from birth forward through early development. The people around you, from your time in utero throughout your childhood, must let you know that you are loved. Abused or abandoned children don't get that, and there are also a myriad of other ways in which a person can fail to develop this basic sense of self-worth.

It's the climactic scene in *Good Will Hunting.* It's not your fault. It's not your fault. It's not your fault. Will's therapist was telling him that the fact that his father abused him was not his fault. Well, what he was really telling him was that the fact that your father abused you, regardless of why or whose fault it was, doesn't change the fundamental fact that you are, as a human being, worthy of being loved, of possessing that most basic sense of self-worth.

The clarity of this point eluded me in 2017 and for much of 2018, too, for that matter. My therapist for his part knew that, for some reason, during my childhood, I did not get this basic feeling of self-worth but could not precisely point to what that reason was. I did keep looking for the big reveal to some degree. My "Rosebud" moment, if you will. That thing somebody somewhere along the way in my childhood had denied me that triggered my loss of self-worth, my loss of faith in the idea that I was worthy of love. If I could find that repressed memory, pull it out, and genuinely reexperience it, then maybe my anxiety would be driven out of me.

This, it eventually turned out, missed the mark slightly. But it did get me to engage in a very helpful exercise. I started talking with my childhood self. I started bringing him along for my walks, and we talked about our childhood. I relived some of our more embarrassing moments and tried to talk through them, tried to remember the shame and embarrassment I had felt at the time.

I had not been abused in any way. My parents were not addicted to drugs or alcohol. This threw my therapist for a time. He probed me for a while about whether my father was an alcoholic or not, convinced that this would explain a lot about my current situation. My father was not an alcoholic.

My earliest days, from my time in utero throughout my childhood, were, in fact, troubled in a series of problematic ways, but nothing as dramatic as abuse or addiction.

This is a crucial point.

Remember, I rejected the idea of needing help for a mental health problem in part because of my belief that nothing that dramatic had ever really happened to me. If you are wrestling with anxiety or depression, please remember this point. You aren't choosing from a specific, limited menu. No physical abuse? Check. No sexual abuse? Check. No problems in the family with addiction? Check. Well, Doc, we're all good to go here, nothing in the mental health department.

It's not that simple.

CHAPTER 20
Understanding My History

My adoption itself was a significant starting point.

Well, I also like to complain that my biological mother didn't know she was pregnant for over four months and smoked and drank more than a little during that time, so maybe my problems started in utero. She spent part of this time on a boat, crossing the Atlantic back to the United States and therefore didn't have much to do other than smoke and drink. She was a code clerk in the US Foreign Service in the

1950s and '60s. I was conceived in Prague, and she, having completed her tour there, was returning for a two-year posting at the State Department in DC.

I was born at George Washington University Hospital in DC, and then spent ten days with my biological mother at what they actually called a home for unwed mothers in Georgetown.

She could not, however, keep both me and her job. The State Department back then would not even employ a married woman, much less a woman with a child out of wedlock. Do not underestimate the depth of our nation's sexism—past and present.

The older of her two older brothers had moved west a little over ten years before I was born, eventually winding up in SeaTac, Washington. He was married with one son, not quite two years old. My biological mother decided to give me up for adoption to this brother. The brother and his wife flew out to DC and picked me up.

What impact did it have on me to have never met my biological father? To have my mother hand me over to two strangers at Washington National Airport and then be flown all the way across the country, unaware that my mother was pretty much out of my life at that point? What was that flight like for my ten-day-old self? Maybe this is why I always get crazy stressed out by the sound of a baby crying? Or maybe it's stressful for pretty much everyone. I don't know. I did discuss the issue with my childhood self during one of our walks, but, of course, neither of us could remember it specifically.

My adoptive father had an anxiety problem he never addressed. But not all the time. He functioned just fine, taking care of the family, but he did have anger issues. Again, he wasn't abusive, just frustrated at times. My adoptive mother had been deeply depressed in her early twenties. She had met my adoptive father because (stay with me here) she was rooming with his other sister in Virginia, and that other sister had stayed with my adoptive mother in large part to stop her from killing herself. My adoptive mother was born in Missouri and moved to Virginia as a child. Born in 1934, she had three brothers and a very problematic relationship with her mother.

My adoptive parents held it together despite these problems, but it all led to an air of instability in my early days. And how did my adoptive mother feel about raising somebody else's child when she had one, and soon two, of her own to raise? I know my adoptive father thought a great deal of his younger sister (my biological mother, not the one who had roomed with my adoptive mother). She in turn worshipped her older brother. My adoptive father must have felt a heavy weight of responsibility to raise his sister's son right.

I never knew any of this until after both of my adoptive parents were dead. I literally grew up not knowing who I was. This, I would imagine, makes it harder to have that well-developed sense of self-worth so necessary in early development.

Then my older brother turned out to be a big problem. *Great, my parents had to have thought on at least some level, the kid in the family who is doing okay in school and is a decent athlete is really somebody else's kid, while our biological son careens out of control.*

My parents' health wasn't great either. I worried a lot in my teenage years about this. They were both overweight and had high blood pressure. I never fully trusted that they were going to be around and healthy for much longer, which, of course, played out exactly as I feared.

Bottom line, it wasn't any one thing, and it's not even clear exactly what part of all of this left me so deeply unsettled in key aspects of my life. I now view it in much the same way I view my problematic hips and my twice-collapsed right lung (it happened again four months after the first time, but we opted for surgery that second time and it seems to have worked). Doctors told me in both cases that the defect—impingement in my hips and something called a bleb in my lung—might have conceivably never caused me a problem. People have impingements and blebs and go their whole lives without ever having hip pain or a collapsed lung. But if the right circumstances combine, then boom, you have a problem. A problem you then have to figure out how to fix.

I refused to accept the idea, presented by my therapist, that my self-worth, me being worthy of love, was a self-evident given —something every human being on the planet possesses merely by being human. I wanted to argue the case. I needed to have proof. I, in an odd way, wanted my life put on trial. I also didn't like my chances in that trial. I had failed—my family growing up and now my family as an adult. The first family fell apart around me, and I couldn't stop it, and now? Now I could barely get out of bed. I used prescription drugs as a crutch. I couldn't get either my anxiety or my physical pain under control. I had a very long list of all the things I couldn't do for my family and to meet the responsibilities of my job. How long before I "lost" both?

I don't think I could have exactly explained what I meant by this. Was my wife going to leave me? My children? Would my entire staff quit all at once? Would I lose reelection in 2018, even though I was functioning slightly better by that point than I had been in 2016? Precise explanation notwithstanding, I felt that impending sense of total failure with the same crushing weight on me as I felt the guilt, anger, regret, and frustration from the way my childhood had gone.

Problem number one on my approach here was that I wanted to correct the past. I didn't just want to understand my history. I wanted to fix it somehow. I would literally imagine scenarios in my head for how my childhood could have gone differently. I had been doing this, on and off, my entire adult life. I imagined my mother never gave me up. She somehow kept her job, and I traveled the world with her, learning multiple languages, and, importantly, being confident in my life, instead of the scared kid I had actually been. I spun many scenarios here. I was in essence trying to erase my childhood self.

It dawned on me, as I tried to have these conversations with my childhood self, that this childhood self would rightly take a dim view of me erasing him from existence. My therapist helped me to slowly accept who I had been as a child. He also helped me to see that blame for what went wrong for me as a child, and for my parents and brothers, really wasn't the point. Life is messy. Bad things happen. Acknowledge them. Understand your history. Grieve for what you have lost. Then live your life.

Do not try to correct the past.

I still wasn't willing to go with him on the whole no-matter-what-you've-done-you-are-worthy-of-love approach, however. It reminded me of a brief flirtation with Buddhism I had back in 2005 during my first anxiety attack. The flirtation ended when I read a book advocating the Buddhist approach. The book explained that love was the key, and we all could not truly experience love until we realized that we had to view everybody as equally worthy of love. I could not bring myself to accept this. It doesn't matter what we do? A serial killer is as worthy of love as my children?

It has to matter, on some level, what we do in this world, doesn't it? If my therapist wanted to tell me, "Don't worry, you are worthy of love because no matter what, you haven't done anything in your life to make you unworthy of love. You know, just like a serial killer," that I wasn't buying.

I will return to this debate later. I certainly don't have any iron-clad answers, but the basic concept is important—whether you want to become a Buddhist or not.

This philosophical debate aside, I still had to deal with the guilt and anger I felt over the debilitating effects of my chronic pain and anxiety, and the drugs I was taking. More than once, as I laid out the case for my uselessness/failure at that point in my life, my therapist would argue the point. "You think you are a failure, likely to be abandoned, because you can't take out the garbage and recycling?" (Doing so involved stairs I could not climb.) "Not a jury in the world would convict you on that. But you've convicted yourself. Why do you think that is?"

We went around and around on issues like this for a long time. My inability to accept that I would not lose everything just because I was physically impaired was driven mostly because of the issues described above—the fact that I didn't get that basic sense of being safe and secure, of being loved, as a child. I still didn't understand this exactly.

Yes, missing this most basic instinct, missing that healthy narcissism, the baseline unconditional understanding that your life has worth no matter what, is a significant problem that I had to address. But looking back on it now, I think there was one other thing nagging at me.

My story, as I keep saying, is not that unusual. It's almost a cliché when stripped down to the basics. Anxious father aside. Depressed mother aside. Adoption. Messed-up older brother. The basics are that I was a child who wanted a different, yes, a better life than the one my family had.

Countless people find themselves in this trap with equally countless variations. You grow up struggling and want something better, but what does that desire say about the lives of your parents? The people who sacrificed to raise you? In my case, who volunteered to make that sacrifice? How dare any child look at his parents and say, you're not good enough for me. That's not actually what the child is saying, of course, and most parents want better lives for their children, but the internal conflict can be tough on a child too young to even begin to grasp concepts like that. That struggle, I imagine, lasts longer when the parents die before the child has a chance to even try to reconcile the issue with them.

I focused on creating my better life as my mother, my father, and my older brother fell apart around me. Engaging in some time-traveling psychological exercise to decide what, if anything, I could have done differently to address these issues is quite beside the point. I wasn't focused on doing anything to fix them. I was focused on surviving the chaos and pursuing the life I wanted. I was focused on me.

Is this okay? Not okay? Does it make me an awful person? I honestly don't think so, but it is something I needed to come to terms with and never did. I also, remember, never understood that the answer to the question does not alter in any respect my fundamental self-worth, that basic self-worth we all have just as human beings. The fact that I didn't know this made the question much more of a threat to my basic mental health as an adult.

But, all that aside, there is one thing I never said, and then never had the chance to say, to my parents. I'm sorry. From the bottom of my heart, I'm sorry. I'm sorry for the bad things that happened to you in your lives, and I'm truly sorry for not having done more to help you when I could have.

CHAPTER 21

Maybe It Just Is
What It Is

My mental health and my physical health had become very difficult to separate at this point. I might have been struggling to understand my history, to grieve for what I had lost, and to not try to correct my past, but I damn sure knew that if I wasn't so physically impaired, I would be better able to deal with all of those things.

My therapist understood this as well. He didn't dismiss my physical symptoms and, in fact, worked closely with me to find a treatment plan for them. This was an improvement over one of the several other psychologists/psychiatrists I had tried previously. He felt I could just put it out of my mind. "Go home and take as long a walk as you want," he told me at the end of one session. He seemed to believe that if he magically convinced me I didn't need to be anxious, then what was stopping me? I did as he suggested and was barely able to walk the next day. I stopped seeing that therapist. The power of positive thinking only goes so far.

But why wasn't I getting better physically? My anxiety and medication may not have been helping, but neither, I thought, fully answered this question.

My extensive utilization of countless physical therapists, personal trainers, and so forth had led me to a straightforward formula—muscles can be lengthened and strengthened. This seemed to be the challenge for me. Every one of these people I saw always started by checking my range of motion and my strength, trying to find the places on my body in both of these areas that appeared to need the most work. This they had no trouble doing. You name it on my lower body—external hip rotation, internal hip rotation, hamstrings, quads, butt muscles, hip flexors—areas in need of greater strength and flexibility were not in short supply.

I worked at it. I stretched. I attempted any exercise I could do to get stronger. Some days, the range of motion would seem to be improving or a particular exercise seemed to be making me stronger. Other days, especially on the range of motion, it would slip backward. Huge setbacks also occurred. Knee pain spiking after some new exercise. My lower back going out to the point where the pain threatened to overwhelm me. My feet cramping up and leaving me in horrific pain, though thankfully only for thirty seconds or so.

I even continued to embrace the muscle release concept promoted in approaches like myofascial release and dry needling. I didn't understand this completely, but if getting stuck with a needle, lying on a lacrosse ball, or using a hard plastic foam roller would somehow make me better? Let's go. Whatever it takes.

The surgeries nagged at me. Did they work? Did something go wrong in one of my hip replacements? Did I need surgery somewhere else? This last thought led to my pointless trips to two different podiatrists, as I wondered about my foot pain and the impact it might be having on my overall recovery effort. These thoughts led me nowhere, however. The hip surgeries were done. There was no way to "fix" them if they hadn't gone as intended. More surgery no longer appealed to me as I was well over a year past my most recent hip replacement and apparently still struggling to recover from that. I did not see the benefit to digging yet another hole out of which I would have to climb.

Could the pain be psychosomatic? Triggered by my anxiety? I asked these questions often, and then I stumbled across a theory that briefly made me focus even more intently on this possibility.

Healing Back Pain, written by Dr. John Sarno, advances the idea that people experience physical pain, in some cases, because of suppressed painful thoughts or experiences. He wrote several other books expanding on this idea. Psychosomatic missed the point, he argued. The pain was real. Our bodies just generated the pain as a distraction, going so far as to actually cut off blood flow to muscle groups that would cause very real, actual physical pain. Why? Because the memories or current worries so distressed us that we couldn't bear to think about them. Don't focus on being abused as a child, or how angry you are now about how your family is treating you. Focus instead on your back pain.

The solution? Understand that there isn't anything actually wrong with you. Ignore the pain. It's a trick. I actually spoke to somebody who had read *Healing Back Pain* and found the theory totally fit his situation. He ignored what he thought was crippling back pain and just decided to go work out aggressively. It worked. The pain went away.

Dr. Sarno also advises psychotherapy. Expose those repressed thoughts. Bring them out into the open and show your body you are not afraid to address the suppressed thoughts, so there's no point in trying to distract you with physical pain.

I'm sure this works for some people. It didn't work for me, and my psychologist had serious reservations about Sarno's approach. Pain can, no doubt, be triggered psychologically. I don't understand how with any depth and would advise you to read Sarno's books and study his theory for yourself. I did realize, as I attempted to convince myself that repressed memories were the source of my pain, that Sarno's advice was very similar to that of the psychiatrist I had already rejected—the one who told me to go take a long walk and just don't think about the pain. The approach didn't work any better this time. My pain remained firmly in place.

Maybe this was just it. I wouldn't get any better. I would have to learn to live with my severe physical limitations.

Maybe I was making too much of it. Many people had it far worse than me. Quite frequently, during this period, I would be feeling particularly down and sorry for myself, walking the halls of Congress or struggling through whatever workout I could manage at the gym or wherever I happened to be at the time.

Then I would see a person far worse off than me. Someone pulling herself out of her wheelchair so that she could do her best to work out on some exercise machine. A person walking in the Rayburn House Office Building, having to propel himself forward with braces on each arm because his legs barely worked. As it happened, I worked closely with a member of Congress who had been permanently confined to a wheelchair since suffering an accidental gunshot wound at the age of nineteen. He made his life work somehow. What was I complaining about?

Here's the thing about that, and my therapist agreed with me on this point: somebody else's pain doesn't reduce yours at all. I had no shoes, saw a man with no feet, right? Okay, I feel really bad for the guy with no feet. But I still don't have any shoes. I did try to find inspiration in people like this, just like I used to look around at people and think about how many of them had to be on some kind of anti-anxiety or antidepression medication. If they can make it, if they can find a way to enjoy their life, then maybe I can, too.

If. Maybe. I just didn't believe it. I didn't believe that there was not something I could do to make the physical part of my body work better.

CHAPTER 22
Everybody Knows a Guy

"Your back's still bothering you?" I answered this not infrequent question in a variety of ways by the time I got to early 2018. This time I went with "Back. Hips. It's a bunch of things. Just can't seem to figure it out."

I stood on the sidelines at one of the fields at the Starfire Soccer Complex in Tukwila, Washington, talking to an old friend I had not seen in a while, as each of our sons played on opposite teams in the game going on in front of us. The cushion on the portable chair next to me and the number of times during the game that I had dropped to the turf on the sidelines to try one stretch or another made it hard to hide that something was still bothering me physically.

"I'm sorry," she said. "My back was really bothering me last year. I found this great therapist in Bellevue. He worked wonders. I can give you his number if you like."

Everybody knows a guy.

What new ideas could this guy possibly have that I had not heard at that point? Stretches. Exercises. Icing strategies. New-fangled pieces of equipment designed to work that one key muscle in just the right way. Foam rollers. Pressure points. Books. Videos. What was the point in chasing after yet another physical therapist?

That March was a particularly low point for me, however. I had, the previous Christmas, in a fit of blind optimism, given to my children as a gift a planned trip to Disneyland for the coming summer. I jumped into the pool and hoped I would figure it out. I didn't. I knew by March there was no way it was going to happen. I still couldn't sit in a chair without being cushioned. Even with the cushion and other protections, I was still in pain. And I couldn't climb stairs. I sure as hell wasn't going to Disneyland. I couldn't just give up, so, after a month of trying to avoid going down yet another road, I texted my friend's guy in Bellevue and set an appointment.

On April 1, 2018, I arrived at the appointment in a lot of pain. The facility was the bottom floor of a three-story warehouse-looking building. Inside it had a lot more workout equipment than any of the previous PT facilities I had seen. It did have five or six of the standard PT tables I had come to know so well, mixed in between the equipment. People were working out on the machines, and others were lying down on some of the tables being treated by what I guessed had to be the PTs who worked there.

I looked at the two hard wooden chairs just inside the front door—there wasn't any kind of lobby, and no obvious place to check in. It pained me just to think about trying to sit down on those chairs. Standing also hurt, however, so I tried walking around a little, acting like I was checking out the equipment. I identified myself when somebody asked, and I told him who I had an appointment with.

"He'll be with you in a minute."

I finally decided to lay down on one of the unoccupied PT tables, pulling myself into a figure-four stretch to try to ease the pain.

"What do we have going on here?" I looked up to see my potential new PT looking down at me skeptically. I hesitated, unsure of what he was asking exactly. "Just trying not to be in pain?" he guessed.

"Well, yeah," I responded.

I prepared myself for the inevitable examination. Internal hip rotation. External hip rotation. Hamstring flexibility. Adductors and abductors. The whole routine. This guy didn't do any of that.

He wasn't even actually a PT. He used to be, but, as he put it, he got tired of not being able to help people. He was now a Muscle Activation Techniques (MAT) therapist, a program started in Denver. He spent the hour of our appointment explaining to me how the program worked while I told him about my exercise routine—all the stretching, foam-rolling exercises I was doing. The epic, three-and-a-half-year battle I had been fighting. My three surgeries. The knee surgery way back when. The various places I hurt. The drugs I was taking.

I didn't fully grasp most of what he was saying. I did get that he was adamantly opposed to stretching and foam-rolling, and I think it physically pained him when I told him what I had been doing with that lacrosse ball.

"Please stop," he said simply.

He listened as I explained my drug intake. "You're taking 2,000 milligrams of Tylenol? Every day?"

"For over three years." I found it interesting that he mentioned the Tylenol, skipping past the tramadol and the clonazepam, among others.

"That has to stop. You need to get to the point where you aren't taking anything. Just messes up your body's ability to heal itself."

I wanted to know if he could "fix me," and if so, how long it would take.

"Can I fix you? I don't know. What we do here is make your body work the way it's supposed to work. There's no set timetable."

We set a two-hour appointment for April 16, about two weeks later.

"Okay," I said. "What should I do between now and then? In terms of exercise."

"Nothing."

"Excuse me?" Asking me to do nothing is like asking a fish not to swim.

"Walk. That should be fine, but don't do anything else. At this point, it won't help."

I followed his advice for the most part, though I did sneak in a couple of workouts, and I returned on the appointment day to get started on the new program.

No, he didn't take insurance.

CHAPTER 23
How Our Muscles Work

How does our incredibly complex muscular/skeletal system actually work? Nobody, at this point in human history, knows every detail of that answer. But we are learning. Some, it turned out, a lot more than others. The MAT folks had done exhaustive studies to figure out how that system worked and are still working on learning more.

It starts with this. There are forty-three distinct muscle patterns in our body—not individual muscles, but patterns, groups of muscles that allow the body to do the movements it does. It helps focus that to understand that ten of those forty-three patterns are in our feet, eight in our hands, and four in our neck.

The other twenty-one are in the rest of our body. They all work together in tandem, and each one is symmetrical, with a right and a left. The better these forty-three patterns are working, the better our entire body is working. Muscles working properly stay flexible and get stronger, thus doing their job to allow the body to move without damaging joints and other parts of our body— like discs in our back, for example, or the muscles themselves for that matter.

How do we know if any or all of these forty-three muscle patterns are working properly? This is where MAT starts. You get up on the table, and the therapist puts your body into a series of different positions, each of which allows him to specifically check if a given muscle group is working.

The physical motion of hip flexion is an easy one to describe. You lie on your back and the therapist lifts one of your legs straight up, bending at the hip with the leg staying straight. He then gently attempts to push the leg back down toward the table. The only way to stop the leg going down at this point is to engage the pattern of muscles that control this specific movement. If it's working properly, that happens—your leg does not go down under the gentle pressure. If not, you are powerless to stop the downward motion. In that case, your hip flexor muscle pattern is "shut down." This is not good. It means that every activity you are doing with your body is having to be done without the full use of this rather important muscle group. Surrounding muscles and joints have to compensate in unnatural ways. This causes pulled muscles, damaged joints, and pain.

MAT started here by developing tests to check muscle function. Interestingly, the body is perfectly symmetrical. If your left hip flexor is shut down, so is your right. Every single time. Thus, even if the activity that overworked or overstretched a given muscle happened on just one side, it doesn't matter. Both shut down.

Next up, what can the therapist do to get that muscle group turned back on? Each function, each of the forty-three muscle patterns, like the hip flexor, involves multiple muscles—some of the forty-three patterns involve more than others. The therapist uses hand massage to turn those muscles back on. It works like a charm. He massages a few muscles and then redoes the test. Every single time I've ever had this done, the muscle in question gets turned back on. The hip flexion test, for example, redone after the very quick muscle massage, instantly stops the downward direction of the leg.

But will it stay on? The therapist then "stresses" the muscle. He stretches it, basically. Again, every single time, this simple stress of the muscle turns it back off. Then back to turning it on with the massage. This pattern gets repeated, usually three times in my experience, until the muscle stays on even after being stressed. This means the muscle will much more likely avoid being turned off when used in exercises or normal physical activity.

My therapist also had me do an odd thing, back when I first started MAT, after stressing the muscle and before turning it back on through massage. I stood on a vibrating platform for twenty seconds and did very gentle squats while holding on to the handles of the machine. The vibrations seemed to help both with turning the muscle back on and building up its tolerance for activity so it would stay turned on. Later, this shifted.

Instead of the vibrating platform, he had me do certain machine exercises that focused on the muscle pattern we were working on. Again, the goal being to build up the tolerance of the muscle for more strenuous activity.

I was a mess when I started this process. I don't recall if every single one of my forty-three patterns were shut down at first, but it was close. We started each session going through the muscle patterns in the same order. It took a couple months until we got through all forty-three and got them all turned back on.

Was this it? Was this the solution to my physical problems? I could not be sure. Initial optimism was not a new experience for me. Just about every physical therapist, personal trainer, and so on had something slightly different about their approach. "No, don't do that exercise; do this exercise." "You're doing that stretch wrong. It's like this." "My massage technique gets after the muscles in a whole different way." "They call me the muscle whisperer." "I'm the person people come to when nothing else has worked." "Myofascial release is a whole different approach. It's been called revolutionary." "Dry needling makes your muscles work like they're supposed to work." I had heard it all. Over and over again.

I liked that my new guy didn't make claims like this. He just went to work. He also didn't seem overly interested in the long, incredibly detailed analysis I liked to do—a feature of all my previous relationships with therapists—usually summarized in epic emails I would send to whoever was working on me at the time. I would analyze every specific aspect of my pain, all the stretches and exercises I was doing, and the medications I was taking. I would detail how a specific pain might be related to some specific exercise, stretch, or activity I had done.

"We don't chase pain," my new therapist said. "We focus on function. Pain in one specific area could be because of loss of function in some different part of your body."

I did notice one thing I hadn't ever experienced before in physical therapy. I felt better after my appointments, not cured by any stretch, but all my previous physical therapy had left me in more pain in the short term. This had been explained as being like the soreness after a good workout, so I didn't know if my being in less pain after MAT was a good thing or not. But I had an inkling that it was.

Other concerns remained, however. First of all, I wasn't getting that much better. I still sat on a cushion all the time. I still needed to lie down quite a bit. Muscles and joints still hurt, even if they seemed to hurt a little bit less. On a scale of one to ten, right? Had I been a seven, and now I was a five? A six? I didn't just go home after a month of MAT and start racing up the hills in my neighborhood. The changes seemed more in the slow-and-steady, two-steps-forward, one-step-back categories than they had been.

My new guy also seemed to think that all these restrictions I had been placing on my physical activity for going on thirty-five years weren't really necessary. This made me nervous. Would my back really be fine if I lay on my stomach, or heaven forbid arched it, or if I sat without back support? How would my knee survive this exercise I had been avoiding for years? And my foot? I had been wearing orthotics for almost ten years at this point and wearing shoes with more and more cushion for support. Not necessary once we got my body back working like it should, he assured me. Less support in my shoes, the better, so my feet could work as intended.

I was still on drugs. My muscles were still horribly atrophied. I still hadn't fully accepted the idea of my own fundamental self-worth as a given. Pain still greatly limited me, and sometimes my new MAT guy was wrong about how quickly my body would be ready to do some of those things I had not allowed it to do for years. But, as I moved into the summer of 2018, I was getting better. More importantly, for the first time, I thought I was working with people who had done the detailed work necessary to truly understand how the mind and the body work.

Mental and physical health problems do all come down to two basic issues—getting the right diagnosis and the right treatment plan.

CHAPTER 24
The Right Diagnoses

had, in essence, two ticking time bombs planted inside of me during my childhood. Well, I guess you could say three if you count the blebs on my right lung. But, knock on wood, that resolved itself with only a manageable level of disruption.

It took a very long time to correctly diagnose those first two ticking time bombs—one being the source of my anxiety, the other the source of my physical pain. Even when initially diagnosed, neither was some kind of *aha!* moment leading to total understanding and a quick resolution of either problem. Not like going, *Oh, look! The lion has a thorn in his paw. Let's just take that out, and all good—now the king of the jungle is my friend and ally for life.*

It took time for me to trust each diagnosis, and the treatment plan for both required a substantial amount of time and effort.

First, on the mental health side, I did not get, for whatever reason, the basic nurturing assurance as a small child that I was worthy of love. I don't think this is necessarily like an on/off switch. The environment any given person grows up in has a level of emotional security that varies. I also imagine that the genetic makeup of a given person can make them more or less susceptible to an insecure environment. But if these things combine to trigger a high level of insecurity in a child, that child becomes more prone to seeing the basic ups and downs of life as existential threats. This can trigger anxiety that equates a failure in life to that homicidal maniac coming at you with a machete.

That's the mental health diagnosis. It took me a long time to get clarity on this diagnosis. I honestly don't know if this was more because of my own blind spots on the issue or because of faults in the healthcare system where I went to find answers to my anxiety.

I do feel strongly on three points. First, our society and our healthcare system do not make it easy to seek mental-health treatment. There needs to be less of a stigma against acknowledging mental-health problems, and a much more seamless way to seek treatment once you do.

Second, there is too much inconsistency in mental-health diagnosis and treatment. Complex mental-health problems no doubt happen to people, but of the ten or so psychologists/psychiatrists I saw, there was no consistency in the basics. My baseline problem of overreacting to the normal stresses of life due to a basic insecurity created during my childhood development is not even remotely unusual. But it wasn't until the last of the therapists I worked with that any of them even mentioned it. Several had focused on the reality that I needed to not be so hard on myself, but the real issue, which I think should have been obvious to any halfway decent therapist, was why I was doing that in the first place.

Third, mental health and medical professionals way overrely on antidepressants and anti-anxiety medication. It is a national disgrace, driven by healthcare providers either too damn lazy to do their jobs, or too trapped in a series of financial incentives that don't give them the space to do their jobs—and by a pharmaceutical industry that puts making money over the health of the people their products are supposed to be helping.

The treatments themselves, once I was given a clear diagnosis, did make a difference. CBT helps. Our minds can run away with unfounded fear. Good to ground that in a realistic look at the percentages. Also, good to make to-do lists and make plans to help ease worries about situations our minds find threatening.

Psychotherapy helps us both understand our history and come to grips with the reality that we cannot correct it. I needed to better deal with my guilt and anger about my relationships with my family growing up. I needed to understand that fantasizing about some different, magical childhood—trying to erase my past—would only lead to me suppressing things I needed to confront. And I needed to better grieve for my parents and what was lost for all of us because of the conflicts within our family unit.

More than anything, however, I had to accept the fact of my basic self-worth as a human being and understand how my upbringing had blocked my natural understanding of this reality. Only then could I blunt the cycle of anger and self-loathing that consumed me every time I thought I had made a mistake or failed. This, to some degree, simply required me to do what my therapist did. He basically made himself my lawyer and then worked to convince me, the jury, of this case. He talked me through it and both helped me understand my history that made me doubt my essential self-worth and gave me better insights into the basic concept that everybody, no matter who they are, is worthy of this fundamental level of love.

Three barriers remained after having made substantial progress on all of the above-listed items. First, my physical pain. It made everything more difficult in general, but more fundamentally, I just sensed more could be done to make it better. This caused a disturbance in my basic being—like driving to the airport and knowing you were forgetting something important but not being able to think of exactly what. Damn, my passport. This forgotten item could still be a big problem, but at least then you knew exactly what the problem was. I knew a better answer to my physical pain was out there, and until I found it, that knowledge made my mental problems more challenging to put to rest.

Second, the drugs. Now, four of the five medications I was taking as 2018 drew to a close were directly for pain, not anxiety, so getting a handle on the physical was also a crucial step on the drug issue. But those four, combined with the anti-anxiety med clonazepam, all stood in the way of my body truly healing itself, mentally as well as physically.

The last issue is harder to explain. Okay, I needed to change my mental outlook. I needed to worry less and stop being so hard on myself. But worry, worry, worry; think, think, think; work, work, work had gotten me pretty far in life. I didn't really want to stop playing at the level I was playing at. How could I still be successful, how could I still be me, if this psychologist convinced me I had to change who I was?

"You won't just be different," he assured me. "You'll be better."

I didn't believe that in the early part of 2019, even with all the progress I was making by that time on both the mental and physical front.

The physical diagnosis also started in my childhood. There were those impinged hips as a starting point. That's a genetic condition. How badly they were impinged is debatable and, depending on the activities one chooses in life, impinged hips frequently don't create any problems. I loved sports, however. Okay, I didn't do something like competitive rowing or downhill skiing that can really grind away on the hip joint, but I was active—playing soccer, basketball, and baseball for most of my young life.

The big problem, however, was not genetic. It started with a simple accident that happened to me when I was twelve years old. A bone died in my knee. How? No way to know for sure. Apparently, if you bang certain parts of your body in just the right way with just the right amount of force you can damage key blood vessels to the point that they stop pumping blood to certain areas. Somewhere along the way, I slid into a base too hard or got tackled on the soccer field in the wrong way or maybe just flopped down on my knees too hard while playing with my friends and damaged a blood vessel around my knee to the point that proper blood flow stopped. The bone in my knee then died.

I felt the weakness in my knee that fall, when I was twelve, and went to the doctor and he gave me this diagnosis. He told me, no sports for a year. I complied, then went back to being active after that one-year break. The knee kept bothering me. and when I was fifteen, the doctor recommended surgery. The details of the surgery aren't important. What's important is that I never properly rehabbed it.

"How long ago was your surgery?" I stared back blankly at the personal trainer, an employee at the LA Fitness where I worked out in Federal Way, Washington. Mostly, I wondered why he was talking to me. I didn't use personal trainers. I went to the gym, did my workout as quickly as possible, and then got back to my busy life as efficiently as I could. It was 2010 when this personal trainer asked that question, and my life was very complicated at that point.

"Your right leg," he explained. "It's atrophied."

"Oh, that. Well . . . " I paused to do the calculation in my head. "Twenty-nine years ago."

I never rehabbed after my surgery on my right knee in 1981. I compensated. This slowly and inevitably made the left side of my lower body much stronger than the right. It pushed my spine over and jammed my pelvis forward. It no doubt aggravated the hell out of those impinged hips and forced me to use muscles—and to not use muscles—in ways my body was never meant to work. It caused almost all of them, by the time I first met my MAT therapist, to shut down to one degree or another.

That's the diagnosis that literally more than a hundred supposed experts in the muscular/skeletal system missed over and over again. Yes, my MRI showed damaged hips, but it also showed my curving spine, my misaligned pelvis, and the basic fact that my entire body was tilted off its axis, pushed forward on the left side. The countless basic examinations I received also clearly showed the weakness in the entire lower-right side of my body. Most missed these things entirely, especially the hip surgeons. Those who did recognize these broader problems, problems that should have made it clear to everybody that I wasn't just rehabbing from hip surgery, then could not come up with a treatment plan to address those problems.

Finally, after years of pain and frustration, the MAT people gave me a treatment plan and helped me implement it, which clearly helped. I am grateful beyond words for this, but it does raise the question of why over a hundred other people, people whose day-in and day-out jobs were to help improve healthcare conditions exactly like mine, completely failed to do so in my case.

Why did this happen?

- Because the human body is incredibly complex and difficult to fully understand.
- Because the human body has an amazing capacity to heal, leading us to believe that something we did fixed a problem with it when it really just fixed itself.
- Because we are all too aware of the things that can go wrong with the body that can't really be fixed, and therefore find it tempting, when we can't solve a problem, to just assume it can't be solved.

- Because the economic incentives in our healthcare system are a massive incentive for healthcare providers to not dig very deeply to find answers to healthcare problems. They stick to what they know and to what they get paid to do.

- Because complex problem-solving requires a skill set very few people possess to the degree necessary to deal with these types of complicated healthcare problems.

But, even in the face of all this, some healthcare providers do dig deeper. They do the work and take advantage of modern technology and the growing amount that we do know about how the body works to find updated, better answers.

This is what the MAT people did. They studied muscles for a very long time as they wrestled with helping patients. They examined cadavers, worked with countless patients, did studies, and ran tests, refusing to accept the idea that it's all just some big mystery we can't figure out.

This extra work gave them the ability to understand that just worrying about lengthening and strengthening muscles left out a key component of the health of our musculoskeletal system. We also have to make sure our forty-three muscle patterns are working properly. This step also helps guide us in knowing if imperfections in, or damage to, our musculoskeletal system really requires a surgical fix. My misuse of my own musculoskeletal system over the course of thirty-five years left me in distinct need of a reboot. Traditional exercises, stretches, and treatments were not going to be able to paper over my structural flaws. I had to get my muscles back working as intended while slowly rebuilding strength in key areas, especially that lower-right portion of my body.

The MAT process has not stopped learning and growing since I first walked into one of their fitness centers back on April 1, 2018. The process of confronting problems as complex as the human musculoskeletal system requires a continuous effort to grow in one's understanding of it. MAT now uses electric pulses to turn the muscles back on instead of manual massage. They had to study for several years to find the exact right frequency, but that pulse now gets the muscles turned back on in seconds, much quicker than the manual approach.

I find the process fascinating and could go on at great length about the details, but that's not the point. The point is the approach they take—the relentless commitment to finding answers and always testing assumptions to learn more.

CHAPTER 25

Problem-Solving 101

know a lot more about political campaigns than I do about health-care treatments, so I will attempt to explain what I mean about how we all should approach problem-solving in those healthcare situations by using an example from my life in politics.

I did develop a plan, back in November of 1988, when I made the rash decision—as a twenty-three-year-old, unemployed, struggling law student who was living at home with his mother—to take on my district's incumbent state senator in the coming 1990 election. I looked it up. One Democrat in our state had beaten a Republican incumbent state senator in the just-concluded 1988 election. She had raised $175,000 to do it, and roughly 90 percent of that money came from five specific sources. Therefore, I needed to convince those five groups that I could win, and then they would give me the same amount of money and I would, therefore, win.

Come on, I had worked on campaigns for about ten years at that point. I knew how to do it, I naively assumed. I just needed to get the money. I spent eighteen months trying to convince those groups that I could win. I failed, miserably. They gave me nothing.

This is the analogous point in most difficult healthcare challenges, when the orthopedic surgeon says something like "Well, some people just take longer to heal after a total hip replacement." Or the physical therapist says, "Sometimes people just have to live with a certain amount of pain. But here, I've had some of my patients try these exercises, and they seem to help."

For whatever reason, I decided to keep trying to actually win. Yes, I likely did that because of the double-edged sword of my childhood fears and insecurities. I had to win. I had to succeed. Because in my mind, it would always be a day-in, day-out open question whether or not I had the right to exist. I had to prove that basic sense of self-worth that most people just take for granted.

Maybe. Or maybe I just hated to lose.

The one thing I did have, that June of 1990 when my campaign plan fell apart, was time. I graduated from law school on

June 9, and my part-time job at a Seattle law firm had ended at about the same time. So I doorbelled. All day, every day. And I thought constantly about my dilemma. There just had to be another way to win. I ran through it in my head. Constantly.

Why did I need all that money in the first place?

Well, dummy, you can't win a campaign without a lot of money. Everybody knows that.

But why? You don't show up at election headquarters on the day of the vote and say to the people certifying election winners, "Here, I've got all this campaign money, more than my opponent," and have them say, "Great, you win." You need votes, not money. The person who gets more votes wins, not the person with the most money.

But the money gets you votes.

How?

Well, you know. It just does. Okay, you spend it on mail. On yard signs. On doorbelling brochures.

Yeah, well, you got me there. But why $175,000?

I did a lot of math at this point. You send mail to the households in the district where registered voters live—at least that was the best way to deliver a campaign message back in 1990 in a state Senate race—and to beat an incumbent you send a whole lot of mail. It's expensive to produce, and it's expensive to mail.

I also scrubbed the hell out of the budget to try to find ways to save money. I knew how to do mail, and what's more I knew a

lot of political hacks—friends I'd met working on all those campaigns over the previous ten years—who would help me produce
it for free. That helped. I whittled the cost of doing mail down a
lot and also found a bunch of other places to save money.

Then I remembered two crucial things. First, the basic principle of every campaign—develop a message and deliver that
message to the people most likely to vote in the election. I
worked constantly to sharpen that message, building on what I
learned from voters at the door. Developing a stronger message
didn't cost anything.

But the key was the last part—the people most likely to
vote in the election. The less mail I had to send out, the less
it would cost. I had no opposition in the primary, and neither
did my Republican opponent. Crucial fact number two was that
Washington State, however, had what they call a jungle primary
back then. We both would appear on the primary ballot and
voters in our state didn't have to pick a party to vote in a
primary. It would be a dry run for the general, but crucially, a dry
run with a lot fewer people voting. A quick look at voter records
showing which voters had voted in which elections made it clear
that only about 12,000 people would vote in the primary (versus around 28,000 in the general), and almost all of them could
clearly be identified as living in roughly 15,000 households. Hit
those 15,000, and sure, some of those households would wind
up having nobody actually vote, but of the people who would
vote? I would hit just about all of them even targeting a much
smaller universe than the roughly 75,000 households in my
district where at least one registered voter lived.

So, I doorbelled those 15,000 households and scraped together enough money—including the $2,500 I borrowed from my credit card—to do a three-piece mail plan to these households.

I gamed the system and got a high-enough percentage of the vote in the primary to convince the big-money people to give to me for the general. I then used the efficiency skills I had learned in the primary to get every last drop of value out of even this increased amount of money.

I love this story for obvious reasons, but the next part is actually more important. I ran for Congress in 1996, and I put into practice a number of lessons I had learned about the art of campaigning based on my 1990 experience. One of the biggest? Target your message to the people who are going to vote. Use rifle shots, not shotgun blasts. Don't waste money arguing your case to the people in the audience, focus on the jury. Why pay to send a piece of mail into a house where nobody was going to vote in my election?

Six times as many people lived in my congressional district in 1996 as did in my senate district in 1990. And a lot higher percentage of registered voters were going to vote in the 1996 general election because it was a presidential election year. The primary didn't matter much this time because the powers that be, the ones with the money, were firmly convinced I could win. I needed a plan to win the general election, which meant I needed a plan to target a reasonably large audience, not the small, focused audience I targeted in 1990.

Mostly, congressional campaigns in the Seattle/Puget Sound area ran television commercials in an attempt to reach such a

large audience. They ran their ads in the Seattle television market. This troubled me for two reasons. First, unlike campaign
mail pieces, I didn't know how to make television commercials.
Nor did I have anybody who would do them for me for free. I
would have to pay a consultant. Second, commercials run in the
Seattle television market are seen by several million people all
over the region. You pay for those commercials an amount based
on this audience size. I did a rough calculation and concluded,
counting the people outside my district in the Seattle television
market and the people inside my district in that market who
either weren't registered to vote or who wouldn't wind up voting, that roughly 80 percent of those eyeballs I would be paying
my hard-raised campaign money to have watch my commercial
would not be voting in my election.

It was the mother of all shotgun blasts. That's insane, I concluded. I'll do targeted mail. No TV. I'm better at this than all
those consultants out there pushing TV commercials just to line
their pockets, right? I outsmarted them in 1990. Why would I
listen to them now?

There's always that fascinating moment when a boss of one
thing or another—member of Congress, CEO, store manager,
political candidate, whatever—announces to the people who
work for him his intention to do something unbelievably idiotic.
What to say, exactly? Now, over the years, I believe I've built
a culture in my team to make sure they have no trouble telling me when they disagree with me, but this was early 1996.
People were still, to some degree, figuring me out. Fortunately,
my team, even back in 1996, found their voice and expressed
their concerns about my plan.

I spent some amount of time, however, stubbornly refusing to agree with them. Again, come on; it's me, right? The architect of that miracle campaign victory back in 1990. I know what I'm doing. My staff did not relent. They knew I was wrong even if I didn't. Sadly, the final decision was mine, so at some point they had to hope I would wake up and pull my head out of my ass.

Then I went out doorbelling in March, shortly after the AFL-CIO had run an independent expenditure TV commercial attacking my Republican incumbent opponent for opposing an increase in the minimum wage. Everybody I met at the door was talking about it.

"I am a moron," I said to myself as I drove home that evening. My God, I grew up here—in a blue-collar suburb just like the ones that made up pretty much all of the district I wanted to represent. Television (and this was true in 1996 for all you youngsters looking at TikTok videos on your smartphone) is king. It's where those people I grew up with would get their information. Who cares where the rest of the pellets go? Some of them will go right into the brains of the people whose votes I need to win.

The lessons to be learned here apply to the world of healthcare in the following way. Most of the people who work in healthcare are smart and successful. Sadly, smart, successful people tend to be very resistant to the idea that they may be wrong about something, or that a new situation is, in fact, different is some crucial ways from a prior situation where that smart, successful person had a very specific success.

That's a problem.

The other problem is all the things I previously listed that do not properly incentivize healthcare providers to truly solve the healthcare problems of their patients to the greatest extent possible.

Some of those things fall into the category of just making it more difficult to find the exact right answer. Take massage, myofascial release, and dry-needling, for example. They were kind of doing what the muscle activation therapy people were doing—put pressure on muscles to make them respond and start working. To wake them up, if you will. But they weren't being very careful about getting the real answers to important questions like *How much pressure? On which muscles? For how long? In combination with which exercises?*

The MAT people did this with incredible intellectual tenacity. And let me assure you, that matters.

It's the difference between a political candidate raising a lot of money and spending it poorly, and one who spends the money effectively. Or a candidate who figures out the exact audience he needs to target, maybe even how to target that audience, but then has a horrible message. Or he has a great message but decides to send it to the wrong people.

The rest of my list of disincentives to healthcare providers getting right answers go more toward the lack of consequences for failing. They get paid either way, remember. They also don't get much of a direct reward for developing new or updating old diagnostic or treatment approaches to make them work better. The body heals itself most of the time, so it's hard to tell the difference for a lot of patients, and if the provider is using insurance, then there is always the risk insurance will decide not to cover some new approach.

Much needs to be done to rework the incentives in our healthcare system.

CHAPTER 26
Relief
APRIL 2019

He's not dead. He's mostly dead.

Okay, going back to my *Princess Bride* analogy, my psychologist and my MAT guy had played the role of Billy Crystal in the movie and stuffed that disgusting-looking apple in my mouth—or educated me on how the body and mind work in my case—but it's not like Wesley just jumped up off the table at that point, ready to go.

Neither did I.

Plus, I had issues coming that I felt would require improvements in my health in a reasonably quick time frame. Mine were not issues as dire as the ones Wesley faced in the movie to be sure. Nobody was out to kill me, and I didn't have to rescue a princess from a castle. I had to win reelection in 2018 while facing a challenge from the left wing of the Democratic Party that had the potential to be problematic. And, if I survived that, it appeared likely that the Democrats would again retake the majority in the House and I would have to figure out some way, in my physically impaired, overly medicated state, to function as the chair of the House Armed Services Committee.

It took about a year from that first appointment in April of 2018 for my body to get back to a place where it started functioning in a significantly better way. I had spent thirty-five years messing it up, after all. Key muscle groups would shut down as I started doing more physical activity, and my MAT guy would have to start them back up again. But I slowly got stronger and more flexible as my muscles started working as intended more and more.

I won reelection without much difficulty: 68–32. Democrats did take back the majority, and I got the chairmanship. More than once, in the first four or five months of 2019, I seriously questioned my physical ability to do that job, but I kept moving forward.

I got off the drugs slowly over a nine-month period. That boat rocked a few times, the tramadol and clonazepam offering the greatest challenges. But I made it. I took my last, little, carefully cut-up clonazepam pill on April 5, 2019. I was completely drug-free at that point and have remained so.

I struggle sometimes to explain exactly how I feel now, after all of this happened to me. I want to be accurate. I don't want to mislead people who may be facing similar mental and/or physical health challenges. Emotionally, I always want to focus on one big aspect about how I feel now. But I also know that if I just did that, I would be doing a disservice to a much more important and much larger truth.

The one big aspect my emotions lead me to is the pure joy I have felt since about the middle of 2019. I have my life back. If I remember my philosophy correctly, from my time with the Jesuits at Fordham, it was the Epicureans who posited the theory that all pleasure is just the absence of pain. Or, put more simply, it's like banging your head against the wall. It feels so good when you stop.

There was an episode of *Cheers,* the 1980s sitcom, in which Sam and Diane are on a private plane for some reason when it appears their pilot has died. Sam and Diane are convinced they are going to die as well, seeing as how they don't know how to fly a plane. But it turns out the pilot was only pretending to be dead. He faked his death, he explains, because, having thought they were going to die, every aspect of Sam and Diane's lives will now be infinitely better. It's his gift to them. They aren't exactly grateful for this gift, but the pilot is fundamentally correct. If you are convinced you will never again be able to enjoy the simple pleasures of life, you will enjoy them even more if you turn out to be wrong.

I certainly experience this often. The mere act of taking an hour-plus walk around the hills of my neighborhood, the Cascade foothills looming not far away, brings a level of joy roughly equivalent to how I felt when I was standing and cheering in the Kingdome back in 1995 during game five of the Mariners' playoff series with the Yankees, and I realized that Griffey was in fact going to score from first on Edgar's double and the Mariners were going to beat the Yankees and advance to the ALCS.

And, yes, I did make it back out on the soccer field with my son.

But I'm not trying to spin a fairy tale here. They all lived happily ever after would be an incredibly misleading way to end my story. I'm only using *The Princess Bride* as an analogy.

The more important and much larger truth is that struggle is always part of life, and the purpose of my story is to show how I learned to better navigate some of the basic, fundamental struggles we all will face in this life in the areas of mental and physical health.

I know my mind and body far better.

Mentally, I still experience stress, of course. I still have a complicated life and a built-in desire to obsess over plotting and planning every aspect of that life. A lifetime of tending toward worry and a compulsion to be perfect didn't just disappear from my psyche. Frustration and anger did not magically and completely disappear from my life, either. I just learned far, far better ways of dealing with all of this, and a better understanding of what in my life led me to be the way I am.

The anger and frustration are far less frequent and far less intense than they had been. I don't have all those unresolved childhood issues trapped inside me, tossing gasoline on the fire every time I miss a traffic light. I've pretty much stopped beating myself up. I still hold myself accountable for my mistakes and failings but from the healthy perspective that those mistakes and failings are part of being human, not some final, conclusive piece of evidence of my lack of worth as a person. I've grown to actually see great benefit in finding out I was wrong in something I did or said. I view it as an opportunity to grow, learn, and improve.

And I am no longer the uncrowned king of regret. I don't replay things over and over in my head, trying to wish they had happened differently. I don't need to. I am now much more willing to accept the world as it is. Well, okay, except for that play in the Super Bowl against New England. I do still replay that from time to time, imagining how if the Seahawks had just given the ball to Lynch, or maybe if Russell hadn't thrown a pass where the corner was obviously getting ready to jump the route, well, then we could have won back-to-back Super Bowls and maybe even, absent the psychological damage from that loss, one or two more. But, as any Seattle sports fan will tell you, that's a special case.

Meditation also wound up helping me, even though I don't actually do any kind of daily practice. I may never achieve a high level of inner peace or consciousness, as more serious practitioners might, but the simple concept of understanding that I don't have to chase after every thought that enters my head has been enormously helpful. I don't do this every day, but I will, with some frequency, practice quick meditation while going about my normal day. I will stop plotting and planning or trying to better understand something I am thinking about and just, while brushing my teeth or in the shower or doing some exercise or on one of my walks, simply pause mentally and notice what is going on in my head and the world around me at that moment. I will notice the sounds, smells, feelings, and thoughts I am experiencing and then just let them go. No judgment.

This process teaches me that that's okay. I don't have to solve every-thing right this moment; in fact, I don't have to solve everything, period. That is an enormously comforting concept.

My psychologist was right. This all didn't just get me back to where I was pre-anxiety; it made me better. I have not lost my drive: that relentless, obsessive desire to succeed, to work through the problems I'm facing and find solutions. But now I am able to do all that without the anger and self-flagellation.

It's much better that way.

Physically, MAT didn't erase all the problems in my body. Almost everybody has some number of issues with their muscular/skeletal/nervous system health, either from genetics or just general wear and tear. I probably have more than most but not as much as some. My spine still bends at the bottom, and my pelvis is still tilted forward on the left. Imbalances exist throughout my body due to all those years of favoring one side over the other.

Pain still comes. My feet cramp. My lower back tweaks, and my right knee starts hurting from time to time. But none of these problems cause me significant or lasting pain now, and they do not restrict my activity hardly at all. I climb as many stairs and hills as I want, and I use both legs while I'm doing it. That's the beauty of MAT. If we get those forty-three muscle patterns working as intended, the strength of that most magnificent human machine greatly reduces the impact of whatever problems we might have.

But it's not a cure-all. It makes it less likely that you will tear your ACL or your Achilles tendon, or that pressure on one part of your body or another will lead to a stress fracture. But if any of those things happen, MAT isn't going to have you out running around your neighborhood. You will need time to heal.

My body is such that if I go full out, I will likely shut down one pattern or another and wind up with back pain or knee pain or pain somewhere else. I, too, am still learning. My MAT guy tries to tell me not to overdo it. "Exercise to the point of fatigue, not beyond." But I tend to want to do as much as possible, and it's not always easy to know what is too much. If I do too much and something shuts down, we get the muscle pattern or patterns in question started back up, and I think through how to moderate my activity to reduce the chances of it happening again.

And, of course, working muscle patterns don't solve every healthcare problem out there. I am aware of the possibility of one of those other problems striking me and then having to educate myself on some other aspect of our basic health.

Now, at least, I have a better understanding both of how to deal with mental-health problems and those health problems that do involve the musculoskeletal system, and of how to work through our very complicated and frustrating healthcare system to get the help I need.

CHAPTER 27
We Are All Worthy of Love

B ut what about the Buddhist point about serial killers being as worthy of love as your own child? My conclusion? Yes, one is as worthy of love as the other. But it matters as much what that doesn't mean as what it does. It doesn't mean we don't hold people accountable for their actions, and it doesn't mean we don't take steps as a society to prevent people like serial killers from harming others.

I do, however, believe that all of us understanding that each of us as individuals and everybody else we deal with in this life is worthy of love is crucial to healing much of what ails our society right now. This is the starting point, and it then needs to be combined with people understanding their own personal history, grieving for what they have lost, and comprehending that the past cannot be corrected to create some perfect world.

Put more simply, we all have to come to terms with our own past and our own present. This process isn't easy in many cases, but it becomes much more difficult without the basic understanding of fundamental self-worth.

Hating yourself isn't healthy. You bounce back and forth between soul-crushing guilt and anger at the idea that the world you live in seems to think you are worthless. That anger pops out in highly unpredictable ways. If you have unresolved anger or guilt over something going on in your life now, or something that happened in your past, that isn't healthy either and creates more anger inside of you. It's also not healthy to hate other people, which is why it is so important to understand not just that this basic self-worth applies to you, but that it also applies to everybody else.

Maybe we can feel comfortable hating serial killers, but it is a very slippery slope. How about your neighbor whose dogs bark all night long? Or the guy driving right on your bumper behind you even though you're going ten miles an hour over the speed limit? Or that person at the coffee shop who doesn't agree with you on the need for single-payer healthcare? Or the people you know who supported

Trump? Or the people you know who didn't support Trump (depending on where you come down on that whole thing)?

If people decide that only some people are deserving of basic worth as human beings, a lot of people will quickly make up their own personal lists of all those people who don't make the cut. It happens all over our country and all over the world, and violence, chaos, and instability inevitably follow.

The bottom line here is that we all need to learn better how to disagree without being disagreeable to the point, far too often, of being hateful. The world is made up of all different kinds of people, people who have differences on just about everything. Judgments and disputes cannot be avoided. But those disputes will be far fewer and far less hateful and intense if we deal with our own issues, and always remember the basic worth of ourselves and all those people with whom we interact.

CHAPTER 28

What Are My Liabilities? What Are My Assets?

The bugger about both mental and physical health problems is that sometimes they aren't that difficult, but other times? They can suck you under in the blink of an eye and leave you constantly feeling like you are gasping for your next breath for what seems like a longer period of time than you can possibly bear. I know many, many people have faced far worse challenges than I have. I only hope that we can all learn, both individually and as a society, how to put ourselves in a better position to address these challenges.

Help exists. I did manage to find it, even though I didn't take the wisest path along the way. I was certainly persistent, a very positive trait in these battles, but I could have been much more thoughtful in how I sought out assistance, chose my healthcare providers, and implemented the ideas they gave me. Live and learn. That is the nature of human existence. You can and will make mistakes along the way when trying to figure out how to address mental or physical health problems.

There is, however, considerable cause for optimism when it comes to working your way through complex healthcare problems. The human race in general, and our country specifically, has never had so many tools at our disposal in our search for answers and solutions. It is far too easy to lose track of this reality when you are gripped by uncontrollable anxiety and/or physical pain. You can become blinded by the seemingly insurmountable impediments to ever being able to feel normal again. Those impediments are all too real, but so are the growing number of options for pathways to getting better.

Just about every challenge I've encountered in life has aspects of this reality—some positive things that can help you accomplish your goals, some negatives that will make it more difficult. I have taken to saying in the world of political campaigns that in any given campaign, you have three things going for you and three things going against you. Your job is to maximize the former and minimize the latter. Wesley, the lead character in my oft-quoted movie, *The Princess Bride*, had a similar take on the challenges he was facing.

Remember that, after being mostly dead, he was given a cure for that ailment, but it did not immediately wake him up. His two compatriots carry his seemingly lifeless body to the gates of the castle, hoping to follow through on the plan to enter the castle and rescue the princess. These are the Billy Crystal character's last words as the three leave his makeshift doctor's office: "Good luck storming the castle."

Wesley opens his eyes for the first time as his two friends survey the castle from the safety of their hiding place behind one of the walls surrounding it. Initially combative and unsure of his surroundings, his friends bring him up to speed on the situation. He understands the goal—rescue the princess. His first question? "What are my liabilities?" Pretty significant, it turns out. There are just the three of them. He's unable to move a muscle in his body—though as they talk, he wiggles a finger and then just barely manages to turn his head. The castle is heavily guarded, and they are not sure where the princess is in the castle.

Wesley is not optimistic about their chances for success after hearing the details of their situation. "Impossible," he concludes. "If I had a month to plan, maybe I could come up with something. But this? Now? It can't be done."

But then he asks the next question: "What are my assets?"

This is the key in many situations. The challenge may seem impossible, but what does it hurt to at least find out what exists in your world that might help you succeed? Wesley's two friends are not without skills for starters. One is incredibly talented

with a sword, and the other, played by Andre the Giant, is incredibly strong. Wesley then counts a wheelbarrow and a large
black cloak as assets, and he cobbles together a plan. In *The Princess Bride*, being a movie, this plan, of course, works. He rescues
the princess, and they all live happily ever after.

I realize, as I wrote earlier, that *The Princess Bride* is just an
analogy, and that real life is not a movie. You can't just write the
script you want. But I stand by this basic formulation. "What are
my liabilities? What are my assets?" Add them up, get creative,
and then try to overcome whatever challenge you are facing or
accomplish whatever goal you have set in your life.

RESOURCES

The following organizations offer helpful information and resources for the treatment of a wide range of mental health issues.

988 Suicide and Crisis Lifeline

Free and confidential support for people in distress, 24/7. Call or text 988.

American Psychological Association (APA)

The American Psychological Association (APA) is the leading scientific and professional organization representing psychology in the United States, with more than 146,000 researchers, educators, clinicians, consultants, and students as its members. Their mission is to promote the advancement, communication, and application of psychological science and knowledge to benefit society and improve lives.

To learn more, visit *www.apa.org.*

Anxiety and Depression Association of America (ADAA)

The ADAA works to prevent, treat, and cure anxiety disorders and depression. ADAA improves the quality of life for those who suffer through evidence-based educational resources, professional practice, and scientific research.

ADAA's promise is to raise awareness about the impact of mental health on physical health, to find new treatments, and one day prevent and cure anxiety, depression, OCD, PTSD, and co-occurring disorders.

For more information, visit *adaa.org*.

Association for Behavioral and Cognitive Therapies (ABCT)

The Association for Behavioral and Cognitive Therapies is an organization that strives to alleviate human suffering through the application of scientific principles. It offers a directory of local member clinicians dedicated to their principles.

For more information, visit *www.abct.org*.

FindTreatment.gov

Millions of Americans have mental and substance use disorders. *FindTreatment.gov* is the confidential and anonymous resource for persons seeking treatment for mental and substance use disorders in the United States and its territories.

Visit *findtreatment.gov*.

The National Institute of Mental Health (NIMH)

The National Institute of Mental Health (NIMH) is the lead federal agency for research on mental disorders. The agency offers authoritative information about mental disorders, a range of related topics, and the latest mental health research.

For more information, visit *www.nimh.nih.gov*.

ৎ

This organization was instrumental in helping me alleviate years of crippling pain.

Muscle Activation Techniques (MAT)

Muscle Activation Techniques (MAT) practitioners have a deep understanding on how isolated muscle function can contribute to the total body integrated system. MAT looks at the integrated system by breaking it down into its isolated parts. Through assessing the function of each individual muscle and its relationship to total body function, MAT is able to address those isolated weaknesses in order to improve total body muscle performance.

To learn more, visit *muscleactivation.com*, write to them at 63 Inverness Dr., Suite 200, Englewood, CO 80112, or call 303-745-4270.

ABOUT
THE AUTHOR

A dam Smith is the member of Congress who represents the 9th District of the State of Washington. He was reelected to his 14th term in 2022 with 71 percent of the vote and has been the top Democrat on the House Armed Services Committee since 2011. He served as chair of the committee from 2018–2022 when the Democrats controlled the majority in the US House of Representatives.

He grew up in SeaTac, Washington, in the center of the district he now represents. His father was a baggage handler at SeaTac airport and his mother was a homemaker. He worked his way through college loading trucks for UPS, earning a BA in political science from Fordham University in 1987. He spent his summers back home in the Seattle area working on political campaigns and doing various jobs to pay the bills. He got his law degree at the University of Washington in 1990, and that same year won election to the Washington State Senate becoming, at twenty-five, the youngest state senator in the country at that time. Smith has been married since 1993 to his wife, Sara, and they have two children, Kendall, age twenty-two, and Jack, age nineteen.

NOTES

NOTES